THE COUPLE'S GUIDE
TO FINANCIAL COMPATIBILITY

the COUPLE'S GUIDE *to* FINANCIAL COMPATIBILITY

AVOID FIGHTS ABOUT SPENDING *and* SAVING
& BUILD *a* HAPPY *and* SECURE FUTURE TOGETHER

JEFF MOTSKE, CFP

Da Capo
∞
LIFE
LONG

A Member of the Perseus Books Group

Designed by Trish Wilkinson
Set in 11.5-point Goudy Old Style STD by the Perseus Books Group

Library of Congress Cataloging-in-Publication Data

Motske, Jeff.
    The couple's guide to financial compatibility : avoid fights about spending and saving— and build a happy and secure future together / Jeff Motske. — First Edition.
        pages   cm
    Includes bibliographical references and index.
ISBN 978-0-7382-1816-8 (paperback) — ISBN 978-0-7382-1817-5 (e-book) 1. Finance, Personal. 2. Parents—Finance, Personal. I. Title.
HG179.M687 2015
332.024—dc 3   2014043950

First Da Capo Press edition 2015
Published by Da Capo Press
A Member of the Perseus Books Group
www.dacapopress.com

Da Capo Press books are available at special discounts for bulk purchases in the U.S. by corporations, institutions, and other organizations. For more information, please contact the Special Markets Department at the Perseus Books Group, 2300 Chestnut Street, Suite 200, Philadelphia, PA 19103, or call (800) 810-4145, ext. 5000, or e-mail special. markets@perseusbooks.com.

10 9 8 7 6 5 4 3 2 1

To my beautiful wife, Kendra—you are amazing.

CONTENTS

PREFACE

The Couple's Guide to Financial Compatibility is about love and money. Or, more specifically, it's about how to have a healthy relationship with both money and your spouse. It's about how to avoid the all-too-common fights regarding spending, saving, investing, and the like. It's about how to build your financial house with the person you love and, perhaps more importantly, how to live happily and harmoniously while doing so.

It's the book every couple needs to read *now* in order to avoid shelling out thousands of dollars in therapy later. As you may well know, the number-one thing couples fight about is money—not laundry, not dishes, not housekeeping, not sex (though it's often used as a bargaining chip) but rather those crisp, green Benjamins. Money matters invariably create conflict, so in order to have a happy marriage, couples must get on the same financial page. Period.

If you're reading this, there's a pretty good chance you're at odds already and that you're in need of an independent ref, a voice of reason who is unbiased and will give you some sensible solutions. That's where I come in.

I've been a financial advisor—which involves lots of relationship counseling!—for over two decades. My team of 150 advisors has helped more than fifty thousand clients around the nation achieve financial independence. Our clients range from couples worth eight dollars to those worth eight figures. Yet no matter their wealth, I am constantly astounded at how little some couples know about their finances. I'll ask a simple question—say, "How much does your partner earn?"—and they'll look at me as if I have five heads.

"We don't talk about money," they'll say, or, "That's not my department."

They—you—are not alone. In a *Reader's Digest* survey of one thousand married couples, 48 percent of wives and 49 percent of husbands said they kept how much they paid for something from their spouses.[1] Interestingly, those with higher incomes lied more about what they spent. The point here is this: many couples don't communicate openly and honestly when it comes to money, no matter how much of it they make!

To say this does not bode well for the relationship is putting it very, very mildly. A 2013 study authored by Jeffrey Dew, Sonya Britt, and Sandra Huston found that one of the best indicators of marital discord is what they call "financial disagreements."[2] Couples who fight about finances once a week are 37 percent *more* likely to get divorced than couples who rarely argue about finances. Those who fight daily are 69 percent more likely to get divorced compared to couples who rarely fight about money.

In his study Dew examined the responses of 4,574 couples surveyed by the National Survey of Families and Households in 1987 and again in 1992. Of all the issues that typically caused disputes—housework, in-laws, spending time together, sex, and money—money disputes were the greatest harbinger of marital unhappiness and, ultimately, divorce.

Financial discord exacts a huge toll on a marriage. Although people commonly get caught up in disagreements over current spending habits, it's the excessive accumulation of debt that becomes an unwelcome stranger in their marital bed. Long before these couples even realize they've been living well beyond their means, the burden of overwhelming debt begins wreaking havoc in their lives, more often than not to the detriment of their relationship.

Many times a lack of communication is to blame. Again and again I hear stories from couples who have no idea how the person they married goes about paying the monthly bills. Or that one spouse owes thousands of dollars in credit card debt. Or, on a more basic level, that one has dreams of traveling the world, whereas the other's goal is to save for retirement. And that's the problem.

Because though couples may talk about whether they're spiritually aligned or how many kids they want or if they'd like to live in the country or the city, they almost never consider their *financial compatibility*. They don't discuss whether their views align on dual-income households, taxes, savings, or making a down payment on a house. And they should. It's far better to figure these things out now so they don't take you by surprise and lead to conflict later in life.

Take my clients Jed and Susie, who fell madly in love when they met five years ago. He's a litigator, and she works as a lawyer for a nonprofit. They married in 2011 and had a baby a year later. After the baby was born Susie wanted to quit her job to be a full-time mom. In *her* mind that was always the plan. Sure, she made a nice salary—though not nearly as much as her husband—but they didn't need the extra income, so staying at home seemed like a wise decision. Not only would she get to be their baby's primary caregiver rather than turning that role over to a virtual stranger, but Susie reasoned that they would save money in expenses she'd otherwise incur for work, such as child care, clothing, dry cleaning, gas, lunches, and so forth.

Susie conveyed her plan to Jed, who, much to her dismay, was completely caught off guard. Why? Because they never bothered to discuss it ahead of time. Jed just made the assumption that Susie would return to work after she had the baby. In *his* mind they could afford outside child care, but more notably, he had grown accustomed to the lifestyle their dual incomes provided. Jed and Susie simply had different expectations about what their lives should look like after the baby was born. They did not see eye to eye on how much money was "enough" or on whether they could afford to live off of just one salary.

And then—oh, yes—there was this surprise: Susie had no idea that Jed still owed about $110,000 in law school debt. She had never bothered to ask him, and he had failed to mention it. Oops.

I am proud to say that I've helped countless married couples, including Jed and Susie, work through their financial disagreements amicably and successfully. In Jed and Susie's case I helped them face the realization that their lifestyle was changing with a little one in the house. They talked things over between them, and *together* decided that having Susie at home was in their family's best interest, so we adjusted their budget accordingly. The nights out to dinner decreased significantly, as did the customary shopping excursions and weekend getaways. They are making inroads toward paying down the student loan debt yet are still managing to contribute to their overall game plan.

Jed and Susie are a classic example of how I *know* that these seemingly irreconcilable issues can be resolved. Similarly I have worked with unmarried couples who ultimately discovered that their differing perspectives made them radically incompatible, and they ended up not moving forward with their relationship, saving them both money and future heartbreak.

Although I am a certified financial planner (CFP) by trade, my actual role is much more comprehensive. It's a friendly mix of coach and therapist. The best advisors are relationship driven. I spend a lot of time with my clients, really getting to know them and learning their individual feelings and perceptions about money. I've been called the Richie Cunningham (a "gee whiz" all-American character from a famous sitcom in the seventies, for those of you too young to recall) of the finance world, as a friend jokingly put it. I value honesty and communication; without them a relationship has zero chance of succeeding. Think about the best sports teams: part of what makes them so great is that they know how to work together. They talk about their next play. They communicate.

By the way, I'm not telling anyone to do anything that I don't do myself. I very much practice what I preach. My wife, Kendra, and I go on weekly dates, but regularly one of them turns into what we call a "Financial Date Night," where we focus on our finances. We might go over budgets, goals, vacation ideas, our children's upcoming activities, plans for the future, or what have you. While this may seem unromantic, the fact that we are on the same "team" when it comes to how we earn, spend, and save our money has been instrumental in keeping our relationship on track and our marriage thriving. We make every effort to keep the lines of communication open. So should you!

That's why I created a financial compatibility quiz, called "War of the Wallets." The way a couple answers these questions will help them identify where they may encounter problems today or down the line. The questions are divided into four areas: lifestyle/ values, risk, trust, and planning. It's the launching pad for couples to start serious discussions about money. I insist both parties take the quiz before I work with them; they need to identify where they agree and where they don't. Furthermore, I insist they *both* attend meetings with me together, as a couple. You'd be surprised how many men try to keep their wives out of financial conversations.

It's amazing the epiphanies that come to my clients after taking this quiz. It is chock-full of important questions couples should address early on in order to achieve a healthy financial relationship in the future. For instance:

- What kind of financial future do we want together?
- How do we align our expectations?
- How do we feel about debt?
- Do you consider yourself a saver or a spender?
- What's your definition of luxury?
- Do we want kids? If so, are we financially ready to have them?

And though retirement may be a long way off for some of you, time does have a way of flying by whether you're having fun or not! So it's important to consider: What does retirement look like to you as an individual and to us as a couple? And even further down the road: How do you want to be remembered?

Couples usually avoid discussing these types of issues with one another for a variety of reasons: bills are boring, credit scores are a snooze, and nothing can be more soul deadening than planning a budget or hammering out how much you need to put into an IRA or a 401(k). Since many couples lack clarity regarding their financial compatibility, they tend to shy away from money talks for fear of initiating an unpleasant conversation. But the truth is that every couple needs to discuss these issues—seriously and honestly. They must regularly address whether they're saving adequately, investing wisely, spending responsibly. Financial interests can change throughout our lives, so we need to make this conversation an ongoing one.

This book is a *What to Expect When You're Expecting* for financial planning, a bible for your fiscal future. If you've ever walked down the aisle—or are preparing to walk down the aisle—no matter how old you are, this book is for you.

Ready? Let's get started.

INTRODUCTION
The War of the Wallets Quiz

A few years ago, after meeting with yet *another* couple who was somewhat careless and cavalier about money, I decided it was time to take action. I devised a simple quiz called "War of the Wallets."[3] The goal of the quiz is to help couples determine their financial compatibility and identify areas where they might have differing approaches to money management.

And by the way, it doesn't matter whether you're currently married; this works for couples who are dating as well. Simply put, it's a good idea to familiarize yourselves with your attitudes toward money. Ladies, are you dating a guy who's constantly asking you to split the dinner bill? Guys, are you dating a woman who is always dressed to the nines, while you only dress to the fives? Then you need to take this quiz! The reality is that, sure, love counts a lot, but it doesn't pay the bills or put food on the table. Ideally you want to find someone you love who is also compatible with you when it comes to money. You might think you can change a person—or "fix" them—but people rarely change: they are who they are. So if your approach to dealing with finances radically differs from one another, you'll have to figure out how to sort through and resolve those differences to make the relationship work. This quiz helps jumpstart the conversations that get you headed in the right direction.

Even if you're the most communicative couple who logs every purchase in a tiny green ledger, I bet there are topics on the quiz you've never addressed because they haven't yet come up. But one day they most certainly will—and you won't be prepared. You'll have different opinions on how to handle them, and let me just say that dealing with problems in the heat of battle is tough. Very tough. My job is to help you avoid that trap.

Lots of couples who have taken the quiz worry about what it means for them in the long run. They fret that if they end up with radically different scores—which is to say, they discover that different things are important to each of them—then it means they're doomed for Splittsville.

Au contraire!

It's entirely possible for couples to be incompatible in certain fiscal areas and succeed in the long run. Opposites attract in relationships, and that applies to finances as well (e.g., you like to keep a budget, but he doesn't; he covets the latest gadgets, but you're content to go without). Those kinds of things can be easily worked out. But it gets a little tougher if he's the sort of person who wants to donate to charitable causes, whereas you're more concerned about saving for retirement. Though you're never going to agree on everything—and that's all right—you *must* agree to communicate.

It's also possible for couples to be wildly compatible in a financial area and still "fail" the quiz. Perhaps you're both crazy spenders who aren't interested in saving anything—you just want to live for today. I see a lot of people who pile up debt on their credit cards and don't save a dime because, after all, YOLO—you only live once! They have a grand old time until the credit cards are maxed out and the bill collectors come a calling. Then the fun *really* begins!

The quiz helps to identify couples such as these and their potential for financial success. It does so through a series of questions that are divided into different sections relating to different aspects of your life. Each question has a compatibly/conflict component. For example, if you both want to dedicate 10 to 15 percent of your income to savings, it means you're completely compatible. If one picks 0 to 5 percent (spender) and the other picks 20 percent or more (saver), well, then, it means you're completely incompatible.

Each question also has a financial success component to it. For instance, couples who commit to saving 15 percent or more of their income will have a happier and healthier financial relationship than those who don't save. The earlier you commit to this basic principle, the sooner financial independence becomes a reality for you as a couple. My definition of financial independence is the day work becomes an option—you don't *have* to go to work; rather, you *choose* to go to work.

For those of you who already have a financial plan, one that is written and well thought out—good! You're way ahead of the average American couple, but you should still take the quiz. Why? Because the quiz brings up topics beyond core financial planning, such as: How are you going to deal with an elderly parent who can't take care of themselves anymore? Who is going to raise your kids if something were to happen to you? Not fun subject matter, but tackling these tough questions head on and planning accordingly brings couples peace of mind.

Open communications early on will lead to less stress and better results later. Trust me! The consequences of ignoring emotionally charged issues until they are upon you can be dire—I've seen it firsthand. Yet with a little discussion and planning, they can be aptly addressed prior to any unforeseen events. The quiz brings these issues to light, but it's up to you to act on them!

As I mentioned, the financial compatibility quiz is broken down into several key categories. Each category contains questions for you to consider as an individual and as part of a couple. They include:

Lifestyle/Values

These questions relate to the way you each want to live your lives: where you want to live, what kind of a home you want to live in, whether you like to travel, how much you like to spend on the latest trends, gadgets, clothes, and so forth. This section explores the following topics:

1. Housing
2. Child care
3. Shopping
4. Travel
5. Entertainment

Risk

Do you think Las Vegas is the greatest place on Earth? Is 85 mph on the freeway too slow for you? Do you wear a belt and suspenders at the same time? If you got a huge windfall, would you spend it on a new sports car or sock it away? These questions address your overall tolerance for risk and cover the following areas:

1. Investing
2. Unexpected money
3. Risk taking
4. Debt

Trust

This should be a no-brainer, but you'd be amazed at how many couples don't talk openly and honestly with one another. We will discuss the following:

1. Financial honesty
2. Frank talk
3. Openness

Planning (the nitty-gritty details)

I'll admit, for many of you this can be as fascinating as, oh, watching paint dry. But like it or not, the following factors are critical to your overall financial well-being.

1. Savings and checking
2. Ratio of savings to spending
3. Budgeting
4. Who's in charge?
5. College funds
6. Retirement

Now that you know what the quiz is all about, it's time to actually roll up your sleeves and *take it*! Remember: honesty is the best policy here. There are no grades and no "right" or "wrong" answers. There are, however, some requirements. To start, I want you and your partner to sit down in separate rooms. Go somewhere quiet and comfortable, where you won't be disturbed and can answer truthfully. Grab a glass of wine or a cup of tea. Relax! And yes, I want you in different rooms deliberately so there's no temptation to cheat!

I've included a copy of the quiz below, but in order to get a compatibility score each of you will need to plug in your answers online. You can do so by going to www.jeffmotske.com. You can even take the quiz on your smartphone!

The purpose of this quiz is to gain information to better advise you and your significant other on your finances and investments.

The two of you should take this quiz separately.

The results will be most useful if you answer the questions honestly.

LIFESTYLE/VALUES

1. Housing: My goal is to:

_____ A.   Continue renting an affordable apartment so I can have money for other things.

_____ B.   Continue renting so I can stay mobile for my career.

_____ C.   Continue renting but move up into a nicer apartment.

_____ D.   Continue renting but save for buying a home.

_____ E.   Buy a home as soon as possible.

_____ F.   Continue owning my current home.

_____ G.   Continue owning but move up to a nicer home.

2. Child care: Whether you currently have or intend to have children, what is your plan for child care?

_____ A.   Our kids are grown up or we don't have any plans for children.

_____ B.   One person has or will quit work to stay home with the children.

_____ C.   One person will work part time in order to care for the children.

_____ D. We will use full-time day care.

_____ E. We will hire a nanny/babysitter.

_____ F. We will use relatives to save costs.

_____ G. It will depend on the costs of child care.

_____ H. We have not decided yet.

3. Elder care: Suppose an older family member (mom, dad, in-laws, etc.) becomes ill and cannot do daily activities without substantial help. What would you do? (Check your primary plan.)

_____ A. Adjust my hours or quit my job to take care of them, even if it lowers my household income.

_____ B. Pay for professional help to come to the house or have an assisted living facility take care of them.

_____ C. Sell their house or liquidate their assets to pay for professional help or an assisted living facility.

_____ D. Share costs for professional help or assisted living facility with other family members.

4. Shopping: Shopping is an activity I view as:

_____ A. An extremely important part of my life that I don't plan to give up

_____ B. An occasional indulgence that must be constrained by budget

_____ C. Something to do on an as-needed basis but not an important part of my life

5. Travel expense: My philosophy on vacations is:

_____ A. Take big, expensive (or frequent) vacations—you only live once.

____ B.   Take modest vacations—I have other needs for my money too.

____ C.   Take inexpensive vacations—they are a big waste of money.

6. Travel financing: I pay for my vacations mainly by:

____ A.   Credit—pay later

____ B.   Credit—but pay off in full

____ C.   Cash—pay in advance

____ D.   Some of each

7. Entertainment: My view on dining out, going to the movies or sporting events, enjoying a night of cocktails and dancing, or other entertainment is:

____ A.   It's a very important part of enjoying life and a necessity for me.

____ B.   I like going out, but I try to watch the cost.

____ C.   An occasional night on the town can be fun, but I am content to stay home most weekends.

____ D.   I'd rather stay home and save the money.

RISK

8. Investing: The stock market is:

____ A.   An excellent place to put our long-term money.

____ B.   An excellent place to put short-term investments to try to make some quick money.

____ C.   Too volatile and we should stay away from it.

____ D.   I do not know enough about the stock market to have an opinion.

9. Unexpected money: If I received a large amount of money out of the blue (e.g., an inheritance), I should (check your primary plan):

_____ A.   Put it into a bank savings account.
_____ B.   Invest in the stock market for my financial future.
_____ C.   Save half and spend the rest.
_____ D.   Spend it for something I've always wanted.
_____ E.   Purchase real estate/income property.
_____ F.   Pay down high interest "bad" debt (e.g., credit cards).

10. Risk taking: When it comes to investing:

_____ A.   I'm willing to take great risks for potentially great rewards.
_____ B.   Some risk is necessary.
_____ C.   It's best to minimize risk and play it safe with investments.
_____ D.   I don't invest because I'm not willing to risk any money I've worked hard for.
_____ E.   I do not understand the risk/reward benefits well enough to know what to do.

11. Credit cards: My philosophy is to:

_____ A.   Use them but always pay off the full balance each month.
_____ B.   Use them to buy things I want and then pay the minimum balance or whatever I can each month.
_____ C.   Use them in emergencies when I do not have enough cash.
_____ D.   Avoid them. I only use cash or debit cards, which comes out of my checking, but not credit cards.

12. Debt: When it comes to debt, which of the following best describes your philosophy?

_____ A.   I am not comfortable with *any* debt.
_____ B.   A little consumer (credit card) debt is not a big deal.
_____ C.   I don't mind having debt because it lets me buy the things I need.
_____ D.   I am only comfortable with debt for major purchases (home, car, school, etc.).

TRUST

13. Combined accounts: We have or intend to have:

_____ A.   Separate checking and savings accounts.
_____ B.   Some combined accounts, like checking, but also some separate accounts, like savings or for individual spending money.
_____ C.   All of our accounts are or will be combined.

14. Spending habits of your significant other: How would you rate your significant other on the statements below about spending habits? Please use the following scale:

(5) Strongly agree   (2) Disagree
(4) Agree   (1) Strongly disagree
(3) Neither agree nor disagree

_____ A.   Only buys the essentials.
_____ B.   Is usually very responsible.
_____ C.   Should treat himself/herself more often.
_____ D.   Allows himself/herself a few small luxuries.
_____ E.   Will occasionally splurge on something big.

___ F.   Sometimes will go a bit over budget.

___ G.   Has a problem controlling spending.

15. Our spending habits compared: How would you compare yourself with your significant other on spending habits?

___ A.   I am more the saver; he/she is more the spender.

___ B.   I am more the spender; he/she is more the saver.

___ C.   We are both savers.

___ D.   We are both spenders.

16. Spending limits: How much money would you feel comfortable spending on a single discretionary purchase (outside of routine purchases like food, gas, household bills, etc.) without first talking it over with your significant other?

___ A.   Up to $50.

___ B.   Up to $200.

___ C.   Up to $500.

___ D.   I never need to check before spending money.

___ E.   We normally discuss all discretionary purchases.

17. Discussing spending habits: How would you rate your ability to discuss spending habits with your significant other? Please use the following scale:

(5) Strongly agree   (2) Disagree

(4) Agree   (1) Strongly disagree

(3) Neither agree nor disagree

___ A.   We talk about our spending habits often.

___ B.   We can have open discussions about our spending habits.

___ C.   We rarely discuss money.

_____ D.   He/she sometimes makes important spending
           decisions without joint discussion.
_____ E.   We sometimes argue about spending habits.
_____ F.   I let him/her make most of the routine spending
           decisions.

18. His/her openness: When it comes to my significant other's
income and assets:

_____ A.   I know exactly how much he/she makes and has.
_____ B.   I have a general idea.
_____ C.   I have no idea, but I wish I did.
_____ D.   I have no idea and I don't care, or it is none of my
           business.

19. My openness: When it comes to my income and assets:

_____ A.   He/she knows exactly what I make and have.
_____ B.   He/she has a general idea.
_____ C.   He/she has no idea but would like to know.
_____ D.   He/she has no idea and doesn't care, or it is none of
           his/her business.

20. Financial honesty: Have you ever tried to hide a purchase
from your significant other?

_____ A.   No, I never hide a purchase.
_____ B.   Once in a while if there is a good reason, but not very
           often.
_____ C.   Only when it's a special surprise for him/her.
_____ D.   Yes, because it avoids arguments.
_____ E.   My purchases are my choices, so there is no need to
           disclose.

PLANNING

21. Saving: What percent of our monthly income should go into a long-term savings account?

_____ A.   0 to 5
_____ B.   6 to 10
_____ C.   11 to 20
_____ D.   21 or more

22. Ratio of savings to spending: Which best describes your philosophy?

_____ A.   Try to spend as little as possible and save for the future.
_____ B.   I like to spend money on things while I can enjoy them rather than wait until I'm old and unable to.
_____ C.   Try to live comfortably but within my means.

23. Saving goals: What is your primary saving and investment goal now? (Check one.)

_____ A.   Buying or upgrading my home
_____ B.   Retirement or financial independence
_____ C.   Education for the children
_____ D.   Other (e.g., car, recreational toys, weddings, etc.)

24. Time horizon: Given my goals, my time horizon for saving and investing is:

_____ A.   Short term—I will need the money within one to two years
_____ B.   Fairly short term—three to five years

_____ C. Intermediate term—five to ten years

_____ D. Long term—ten to twenty years

_____ E. Very long term—more than twenty years

25. Budgeting: When it comes to budgeting, I:

_____ A. Keep detailed records that track all my income and expenditures.

_____ B. Try to set a monthly budget but have a hard time following it.

_____ C. Don't keep a budget, but I have a general idea about how much I can spend each month based on my income.

_____ D. I do not currently use budgets, but I know I should.

26. Who's in charge? When it comes to dividing financial responsibilities, who is primarily in charge of:

_____ A. Managing the checkbook, paying the bills, keeping track of the family money, and so forth
  i. Mostly me
  ii. Mostly my significant other
  iii. Both equally

_____ B. Deciding on savings and investments
  i. Mostly me
  ii. Mostly my significant other
  iii. Both equally

_____ C. Deciding on major purchases
  i. Mostly me
  ii. Mostly my significant other
  iii. Both equally

27. College funds: When should we start saving for our current or future children's college fund?

_____ A. Our kids are grown up or we don't have any plans for children.

_____ B. Right away—there's no time to waste.

_____ C. When they are born.

_____ D. By the time they are ten years old.

_____ E. They should pay for their own college.

_____ F. They should take advantage of financial aid and student loan packages.

28. Charitable giving: What percentage of your yearly income do you give to charity?

_____ A. None

_____ B. 1 to 5

_____ C. 6 to 10

_____ D. More than 10

29. Retirement activities: When I retire I want to spend my time (check your primary plan):

_____ A. Seeing the world—visit all the places on my "bucket list."

_____ B. Volunteering in the community in areas that are important to me.

_____ C. Staying home, relaxing, sleeping in, and spending time with my spouse and family.

_____ D. Taking up a new activity that I have always wanted to do but never had the time for.

_____ E. I don't ever plan on retiring—I love my work and plan on working indefinitely.

30. Retirement financial goals: How much money will you need in your retirement?

_____ A. Assuming good health, I want to plan to have enough to live it up.

_____ B. I need enough to live comfortably, with a nest egg for emergencies.

_____ C. My main goal is to not run out of money before I die.

_____ D. I have not given it much thought or planning yet.

31. Retirement financial plan: Our strategy for financing our golden years will rely _primarily_ on:

_____ A. An individual retirement plan, including 401(k) plans

_____ B. Social Security and any other money we are able to save

_____ C. Government or company pension plan

_____ D. Continuing to work part time in a "fun" job for a little extra income

32. Retirement plan progress: When it comes to planning for retirement, I believe:

_____ A. We are saving adequately for a comfortable retirement.

_____ B. We are ahead of schedule.

_____ C. We are behind schedule.

_____ D. We do not know whether we are ahead or behind.

_____ E. We are already retired.

33. Estate/legacy plans: When I die (check your primary plan):

_____ A. I want to leave a legacy and give my money to charities I believe in.

_____ B.   I want to will money to my family so they can have a "leg up" from where I started.

_____ C.   A good estate plan (living trust) is a wise technique to ensure my intentions are carried out after my death.

_____ D.   I do not have a plan—have not thought much about it.

_____ E.   I would like to spend most of my money before I die—after all, you can't take it with you.

34. Retirement planning knowledge: How would you rate yourself on the following statements about retirement planning? Please use the following scale:

(5) Strongly agree   (2) Disagree

(4) Agree   (1) Strongly disagree

(3) Neither agree nor disagree

_____ A.   I know the basics about the various types of investments.

_____ B.   My friends and relatives often come to me for financial advice.

_____ C.   My spouse knows more about financial planning than I do.

_____ D.   I am a little worried about whether my current plans will ensure enough to retire.

_____ E.   I would like to plan to retire at the earliest possible date.

_____ F.   I am not sure of my financial plans for retirement.

_____ G.   I want to avoid risk in my retirement savings plan.

Okay! Whew! You did it. Congrats. Take a sip of wine. That wasn't so bad, was it?

HOW DO WE CREATE A GAME PLAN FOR FINANCIAL SUCCESS?

Now that you've taken the test and identified your problem areas, what's next?

This section is all about creating a game plan for your future, one that is dedicated to your joint financial success.

One of the best times to do this is during a monthly Financial Date Night. As I said, my wife and I go on weekly dates, and one of them each month is dedicated primarily to money matters. During these outings we have a very specific agenda. And while you may think this is excruciatingly boring, we usually do this over a fabulous meal at our favorite Italian restaurant, with a bottle of red wine.

Kendra and I have been married for twenty years (with two teenage kids!), so our concerns may differ from yours. But one thing I do know: most couples don't regularly talk about their financial game plan.

Here's how it usually goes when couples come to me and I ask about their financial plan: "We already have one," they say.

"Terrific!" I reply. "Let's go over it."

That's when the fun begins. They hem and haw. They sputter and mutter. They can't actually provide a written document—or anything tangible. But they swear they have a plan in place in their heads. Sorry to say, but having a plan in your head does not count! Having an individual plan does not count! Having a plan that you have never discussed with your spouse does not count! Having a plan that has not been reviewed and updated on a regular basis does not count!

Then there are clients who say they can't possibly draw up a financial plan because they don't have any money. To them I say: wrong! Everyone has a starting point. You could have significant net worth or you could be in debt up the wazoo. I don't really care where you are. The important thing is to recognize that in order to get ahead in life or even get started in the right direction you must have a game plan for success.

One of my favorite books, 5: *Where Will You Be Five Years From Today?*, a lovely little gem by Dan Zadra, is not just about dollars and cents but about the bigger things in life.[4] The author asks really probing questions: Where do you see yourself in five years? Ten? Twenty? Where do you want to live? In what kind of house? Where would you like to travel? What kinds of things do you want to accomplish? And so on. It's not so much that I want to live in the future—I'm all about enjoying the present—but I do believe in aspirations. Without aspirations—goals, dreams, ambitions, hopes, wishes, whatever you want to call them—life has no purpose. But in order to reach those dreams you have to *plan*. They won't just materialize without a detailed game plan in place.

An advisor and friend of mine from Louisville, Kentucky, Ron Butt, often reminds his clients that "those who aim at nothing will surely hit it!"

Poetic, I think, and true.

This brings me to another question: How do you define success? The definition differs for everyone. Some people think success is about Rolex watches and Porsches. Others think it's about a mortgage-free home. Still others think it's about a strong work ethic or a tight-knit family. The key here is to define success as a couple.

Let me stress again: if you're really serious about getting your financial house in order, you need to take it seriously. You need to treat it like a job. It's for your own good. It will help prevent future arguments and misunderstandings with your beloved—*before* they pop up.

When I think about the importance of planning I often think of my client Alice, who came to me in 1997, hopeless and despondent. Alice was a grocery store clerk when her husband, Roger, dropped dead from a heart attack. She earned a mere $1,500 a month at the time. I met her shortly after Roger's death. As a couple they had never talked about money, and she knew nothing about their finances; only later did she discover that he had hidden about $10,000 worth of credit card expenses from her. Had they taken the quiz—or had they come to me together, before Roger passed away—Alice might have found herself in a healthier financial situation.

Like many people in this country, Alice was embarrassed and ashamed that in her late fifties she wasn't farther ahead in life financially. She had nothing but her hourly job—no life insurance, no pension, no plan. So we set up a budget and discovered that she could take $25 a month from her checking account and put it into a mutual fund. I taught her how to utilize her company 401(k) retirement plan that had a match component to it. We started with 6 percent out of her paycheck, and the store matched her contribution with an additional 3 percent. (*Note:* if your company has a matching program, then you need to contribute up to at least the matching amount—more on this when we delve into retirement.) We reviewed her mutual fund account and 401(k) on a regular basis. (This should be done annually, at a minimum!) Alice diligently saved into this plan and increased her monthly amount as she received raises at work. Over time she created a nice nest egg for herself.

Alice would often say, "I don't know why you're helping me—I have no money." But I liked her. I wanted to help her, and she needed my help. Sure, I wish she had come to me earlier, but the lesson here is this: no matter how much you have or earn, it's never too early to get a plan started. As the saying goes, "Never put off till tomorrow what you can do today." This is especially true when it comes to money.

Another reason to create a plan: it gives you a path to follow together. It creates motivation for you as a couple to go the extra mile. With a shared goal in place you'll likely think twice before spending frivolously. The "family goals" will take precedence over your individual whims.

Three years into our relationship, for example, Kendra and I made the decision that when we had kids she would stay at home and I would work. We both grew up with stay-at-home moms, and that's the childhood experience we wanted to provide for our own kids. We made financial decisions and sacrifices along the way with that objective in mind. It so happened that this was an area in which we both agreed, and we worked in tandem to make our goal a reality. We communicated in advance, made a plan, and stuck to it. For couples who have yet to broach subjects like these, ones that ultimately affect your overall game plan, the quiz works to reveal your financial attitudes, beliefs, and opinions on a whole host of topics. This lays the groundwork for open and honest discussions, which, in turn, leads to creating an effective financial game plan together.

FIRST THINGS FIRST: YOU MUST ESTABLISH A BUDGET

Ah, the dreaded B word. *Budget* has a negative association for so many couples, especially those who are spenders. I understand it:

a budget—a living, breathing testament to your spending habits. Most couples don't do a formal budget, but I insist on it. In fact, it's one of the prerequisites for working with me. You can't get ahead without a budget: it provides structure, establishes direction, and creates accountability. It's essential to the success of your overall game plan.

Even if numbers terrify you and you'd rather grout your bathroom than calculate expenses, you must do it. Think of a budget as a road map, a numerical guide to a financially safe future, the foundation for sound decision making.

Take, for instance, my clients Christine and Jim, who are both teachers in their late forties. They came to me about fifteen years ago for advice regarding a small but significant amount of credit card debt. I helped them understand that in order to eliminate the debt they needed to get their spending under control. Neither one was especially concerned with tracking their expenses, but I insisted. So we did a budget. Today they're a Quicken couple. Jim runs the family budget; he tracks every dollar that's spent in that household, each and every month. Christine is diligent in giving Jim all of her receipts, and now they are much more mindful of their spending.

And by the way, this newfound diligence has only enhanced their relationship. They are a happier couple now. They have a game plan for their future. They both feel they are invested in their union.

For the record, you don't have to use a fancy accounting program like Quicken to tally your expenses. It doesn't matter if you add them up on a computer spreadsheet, a yellow legal pad, or use a green ledger sheet like Kendra and I do—just so long as you do it!

If you've never made a budget before and don't know where to begin, don't worry. In the back of the book I've included a sample budget worksheet that I use with my clients. Generally speaking, you're going to need to tabulate your household income and expenses, which will require gathering any and all billing, credit card, and bank statements. The goal here is simply to get the numbers down in black and white, which becomes the basis for your financial game plan.

BUDGET + 911 FUND + GOALS + PROTECTION = FINANCIAL GAME PLAN

I look at creating a financial game plan much like building your own custom house. You start from the ground up, beginning with a good piece of land and a solid foundation on top of it. Think of your *land* as the *income/revenue* piece of your budget. This should include every dime that comes into the family household on a monthly basis.

Next comes the *foundation*, which makes up the *critical expenses* part of your budget, the absolute non-negotiables—food/medical, housing, and transportation expenses. We are not talking about luxuries here. You have to pay these come hell or high water! They are the footing upon which you will build the rest of your financial house:

Food/medical—groceries, prescriptions, health insurance
Housing—mortgage/rent, insurance, taxes, utilities
Transportation—car payment, insurance, gas, public
    transportation

Atop the foundation goes the *flooring*, an additional layer of your financial house that comprises all your remaining expenses. This is what I refer to as the *lifestyle expenses* section of your budget.

Insurance—life, disability, long-term care
Debt payments—student loans, credit card, other

Dining—eating out, coffee and bar, luxury grocery items
Technology—cell phone, cable, Internet
Personal well-being—clothing, grooming, gym, hobbies,
   vacations
Entertainment—tickets, shows, games, memberships,
   subscriptions
Home maintenance—housekeeper, gardener, pool,
   snow removal
Family—child care, education, gifts, pet care
Other—charity, tithing, fun money

Now that you have your foundation (critical expenses) and your flooring (lifestyle expenses) laid, let's move on to the next phase: constructing the *walls*—your emergency "911 Fund." When you build a house, you want sturdy walls that will hold up in case disaster strikes; the same can be said of your 911 Fund. A solid 911 Fund should eventually include anywhere from three to six months of your critical expenses. So if, after completing your budget worksheet, you determine you have $6,000 of critical monthly expenditures, then your emergency fund balance should be between $18,000 and $36,000. Remember, the stronger your 911 Fund, the better prepared you are to withstand life's unforeseen events.

Now, for those of you who are currently living paycheck to paycheck or have no savings at all, don't panic! You are going to erect the walls of your financial house in stages. Start by accumulating *one* month of your critical expenses in your 911 Fund. You now have walls, albeit thin ones, in need of insulation. Next, aim for three months' worth—sturdy walls with good insulation that will allow you to begin building the rooms inside your house (more on that in a minute). Finally, work up to saving six months of expenses, which is excellent! This gives you a solid framework that can successfully weather a severe storm or natural disaster.

Note: I tell most clients they should have six months of their critical expenses socked away, especially those with sporadic incomes such as realtors or freelance writers. If, however, you've got a good, stable job and steady income—say, you're a tenured teacher or fireman—then three months should suffice.

WHAT'S THE BETTER INVESTMENT VEHICLE FOR OUR 911 FUND—A CHECKING OR SAVINGS ACCOUNT?

You'll want to use a checking account to run the day-to-day operations of your financial house. It's the money that goes toward paying your bills and can be easily accessed for cash purposes. I suggest keeping a minimal balance in this account. You don't want your checks to bounce, but you don't want to keep $100,000 in a checking account either. There's no point—and no interest. It should be utilized strictly for cash-flow purposes.

A savings or money market account is the better investment vehicle for your 911 Fund. Much like a checking account, you'll still have instant access to your cash, but a savings account pays you a fixed interest rate on the money inside it. So your 911 Fund will earn interest, yet it won't be subject to any market risk like it would inside a mutual fund or other such vehicle. You certainly don't want to roll the dice with your 911 Fund, because you never know when you're going to need it.

SHOULD WE SET UP THESE ACCOUNTS JOINTLY?

Yes, yes, yes! The goal here is to work together. So, yes, everything should be done jointly. However—and this is a big however—I also think it's important for couples to have their own individual accounts where they can set aside some extra cash just for themselves. It's important to maintain some sense of independence and individuality, so long as you remain honest and transparent with your spouse.

PROTECTING OUR HOUSE AND BUILDING OUR ROOMS (GOALS)

Now that you have a nice piece of land, a solid foundation, good flooring, and some sturdy walls, what next? Well, it's time to put a *roof* on your financial house. The roof offers you protection; it represents all the *insurances* and planning necessary to safeguard your family:

Insurance—life, disability, long-term care, health
Planning—tax, estate

Once you have the exterior of your financial house completed, you need to get to work on the inside. You want to start by building out the *rooms*; these represent your *primary goals*, which can vary from household to household. Some of the biggies are:

Retirement—early would be nice
Saving for a house—or upgrading your existing home
College planning—if you have kids

Think of these goals as essential rooms in your house. For example, every house needs a kitchen, a bathroom, a bedroom. The money to build out these rooms derives from the **pay yourself first principle**; it's the portion of your budget dedicated to regularly saving money. As a rule of thumb, it's wise to devote at least 15 percent or more of your gross monthly income (paycheck before taxes) to savings. Initially this "pay yourself first" money goes toward establishing your 911 Fund. Once that is set up, these dollars can then be allocated to funding your primary goals.

Treat the "pay yourself first" principle as you would any ordinary bill that you pay on a monthly basis, and before long you'll have a nice little chunk of change socked away. Kendra and I have a fixed amount automatically withdrawn from our checking account each month that goes directly toward our primary goals; this money is outta sight, outta mind, straight into the rooms of our financial house.

Incidentally, how did you and your spouse answer the savings rate question on the quiz? If you both picked 15 percent or more—nice work! You are on the same page with the "pay yourself first" principle. If not, then it's time to have a serious discussion about working up to a 15 percent savings rate. The road to financial independence begins with a well-funded game plan.

In order to put the "pay yourself first" principle into action you may have to find ways to save more and spend less each month. Obviously you can save money by cutting back on certain expenses, like renting a smaller place, buying a less expensive car, or taking fewer trips. But where are you going to find the drive, desire, and discipline to make these budgetary changes? This is the time to focus on the one goal that you, as a couple, are most determined to accomplish. For example, let's say you desperately want a new house. If you want it badly enough and it's stated quite clearly in your budget, then that goal will motivate you to adjust your spending habits—to resist the temptation of that new big screen or handbag hanging in the window. With a clear-cut goal in place you'll spend more wisely and less impulsively.

Reducing the seemingly insignificant purchases can add up to substantial savings as well. Take Starbucks: if you go there a few days a week for one of their super-special lattes, it could end up costing you around $1,500 a year. That's $1,500 that you could put toward a renovation or a vacation or in the bank for retirement. You could brew your own cappuccino at home for a mere $250 a year instead.

Another gem for saving money is "don't be list-less." I'm not talking about the lethargic person who needs a 5-Hour Energy Drink to get through the day; I am talking about shopping without a list. Ever notice that when you shop without a list you leave with a cart full of things you had no intention of buying when you entered the store? Yet we tell ourselves, "Look at all the money I saved because it was on sale!" Literally billions of dollars are spent every year on impulse purchases often from eye-catching displays that entice "list-less" or "window" shoppers.

The same goes for shopping with your kids who want everything they see. If you go to the grocery store without a concise list of items you need, chances are you'll spend way more money than you would have if you had gone shopping with one. A budgeter would never buy junk she doesn't need; she will stick to her list and not go off budget.

Remember, now that you have a budget it means that both of you need to actually track your spending. I suggest a monthly date, like the one Kendra and I have. During this time you can discuss how far along you are in working toward your goals. Also, talk over any planned expenses you may have; you can then adjust your goals as needed.

WHAT NEXT?

You may be saying, "Okay Jeff, we agree we can save, and we are motivated to reach our primary goals, but what about upgrading our financial house?" You can look at upgrading your appliances (increasing the annual vacation fund), switching to granite countertops from Formica (buying an RV or boat), replacing the linoleum with hardwood flooring (starting a wedding fund). You can even put an addition onto your house (early retirement). Cool!

When you consider doing an *upgrade* the first thing you must do is reexamine your budget to determine how you are going to fund it. Did you receive an inheritance or a gift? Did you get a raise at work? Are you going to use your annual bonus, and if so, is that annual bonus consistent?

Imagine, for example, you get a nice bonus this year and decide to buy a boat. What if, however, that bonus isn't handed out again next year? You still have all the costs associated with the boat—repairs, maintenance, storage, and so forth—but not the additional income to pay for it. What now? Do you go into debt trying to fund your upgrade? Bad move, Captain. This is how couples wind up with added expenses they simply can't afford. To make matters worse, let's assume the boat purchase was your idea, one that your first mate was never hip to from the get-go. How much fun are you going to have out on the open waters together when the boat remains a constant sore spot between you? Especially when your mutinous mate insists on renaming it "The Moneypit!"

I might have just made you think twice about buying a boat, but I don't want to discourage you from upgrading your financial house entirely. I just want you to carefully consider your upgrades before you commit dollars to them. Whether you want to increase your vacation budget or create a wedding fund for you daughter, ask yourself: Does this make sense in the overall design of our financial house? If it fits in your budget and you both say yes, then go for it! I think it's important to have these personally rewarding objectives in your game plan; you work hard for your money, so you and your family should reap the rewards of that hard work. My motto is: "Dream big, work hard, laugh often!" You set a goal, work hard to make it a reality, and enjoy it to the fullest once you've reached it.

Creating a game plan will require some thoughtful communication between you and your spouse. And though it doesn't need to be fancy in the beginning, it *does* need to be written down. Putting it in writing turns those thoughts into a tangible plan of action. You would never build a house without blueprints. Think of your written game plan as your blueprint to financial independence, your game plan for success. Place it in a spot where you and your spouse will see it often, even if it's smack-dab in the middle of your refrigerator! Putting a game plan in writing and viewing it on a regular basis are the first steps toward making your dreams a reality.

2

WE MADE A BUDGET AND WANT TO START ON OUR GAME PLAN . . . SO WHY DON'T WE HAVE ANY MONEY?

That, my friends, is the million-dollar question. Sadly, you are not alone. According to Bankrate.com, over 75 percent of Americans live paycheck to paycheck.[5] That means that three-quarters of the public are basically subsisting above their means. In an ideal world, of course, you would receive your paycheck and somehow manage to sock a portion of it away every month (say, 10 to 20 percent)—the "pay yourself first" principle! Admittedly that is easier said than done for couples who are living on the edge without a game plan.

So why are you struggling so much? Well, unless you are very, very poor, chances are someone in your household is a habitual spender. So all those plans that you've been making, all those lists and budgets and spreadsheets—one or both of you is paying them scant attention. It may not be intentional. It could be you are accidentally spending a little more than was allotted in the budget. Maybe you're throwing an elaborate birthday party and are going slightly overboard. Perhaps you've been frequenting that hot new sushi restaurant a few too many times. Whatever the reason, now is the time for a good heart to heart.

The name of the game is *financial transparency*. That means sitting with your bank statements, your credit card bills, your paychecks—much as you did when you first formed your budget—and airing it all out. During this time you *need* to be open and honest with one another. Admit to past errors in judgment. Tell your partner whether you're feeling particularly challenged sticking to the budget. But keep your cool—huffing and puffing will only serve to blow your financial house down, not build it up. You're simply trying to reach some common ground here.

WHAT DO WE LOOK FOR IN OUR BANK STATEMENTS?

When reviewing your bank statements to identify spending habits the biggest culprit is often the use of debit cards. Sometimes there are big-ticket items, but usually it is all the "little swipes" that add up. A smart way to combat those "little swipes" is to give yourselves a monthly cash allowance that is moderately lower than your monthly debit card charges. Then *no* swipes—*cash* only please!

Note on using debit cards: Besides the swipes, which often result in increased spending, there is a tremendous amount of fraud involving debit cards. My brother-in-law is a police detective, and he advises people not to use them *at all*. If criminals get ahold of your debit card or its vital information they can drain your entire bank account in an instant. Imagine your checking account or your 911 Fund being wiped out overnight. The cash you use to pay your bills and run your household . . . GONE! You are then left to your own devices—haggling with your bank or law enforcement in an effort to get your money back. What a pain in the you-know-what! This can't happen if you are making cash-only purchases. Incidentally, credit cards provide better fraud protection than debit cards for those of you who are chronic swipers. But you can probably hazard a guess as to my opinion about excessive credit card swiping!

Automatic account drafts are the other items to look out for when pouring over your bank statements. These are the oft-forgotten drafts that are withdrawn from your account on a monthly basis—are you still getting value from them? If not, perhaps that money could be redeployed into your game plan for better use.

WHOSE DEBT IS IT ANYWAY?

Many couples I meet with have their own personal credit cards and then a joint card to use with their spouse. Their rationale is that they want to have private accounts so they can buy whatever they please.

I get it. Truly I do. But, as the saying goes, "There's no 'I' in team." Remember, the focus here is on you as a couple: you're a team, a unit working to build a better life *together*. When you have your own credit card, it's that much easier to hide purchases and, ultimately, incur debt. For this reason I advise against it. Both names should be on all the cards, and both of you should review the monthly statements.

Here's another sad fact: almost every kind of debt your partner incurs during your marriage is the responsibility of both of you. If you split up and your spouse owes $70,000 in debt, you're very likely going to be responsible for it as well. And if your spouse chooses not to pay that debt, you're liable for it. So it's to your benefit to know exactly how much is being spent each month.

Caveat: I do think it's important to have your own bit of fun money to spend on yourself. It can be "secret" only in the sense that you don't have to clear your purchases with your spouse. Expenditures should be income appropriate. If you make $50,000 a year, your monthly fun money should be about $50 per person—ideally in cash. If you make $150,000 a year, then $150 per person each month is reasonable, and so on. That's money to spend as you wish at your own discretion.

HOW DO WE GET OUT OF CREDIT CARD DEBT?

The easiest way to discern how you have gone astray is by going over your credit card statements.

The good news: it's completely possible to eradicate debt.

The (slightly) bad news: it will require some sacrifice and a willingness to live *lower* than your means for a while. This sounds rather ominous, but it's not—it's just realistic.

I look at credit card debt in four phases: mild, bad, terrible, and deadly. It is more than just the number on the bottom of your monthly statement; it's also a function of your ability to pay it back. So although $3,000 may seem like a sea of credit card debt to an unemployed college student, it is merely a drop in the bucket to a dual-income family of four. It's all relative: The higher your income and the lower your expenses, the more opportunity you have to pay down your debt.

Your budget will help determine what debt phase you are in because it allows you to see the whole picture. Pay particular attention to the Lifestyle Expenses, or Flooring, section when diagnosing the severity of your credit card debt. The sooner you ascertain as a couple where you fall on the debt spectrum, the sooner you can root out the causes and fix the cracks in your flooring, ultimately solidifying the footing of your financial house.

Let's take a look at Rob and Marcia, my **Phase One: Mild Debt** clients. This thirty-something couple had been married six years.

She was a children's book author, and he was an engineer. They had purchased a new home a few years earlier and had gradually been making improvements to it. In the process they had amassed $15,000 in credit card debt. This worried them.

"You say to yourself, 'This is a short-term issue; I'll fix it,'" said Rob. "Yet we make the monthly minimum payments and aren't getting anywhere."

I nodded in understanding. Clearly Rob and Marcia needed to get control of their debt before it morphed into an unwieldy monster.

I know many people who have cut up their credit cards and tossed them in the garbage. While that's a good way to eliminate plastic from your life, I prefer another method. Take your credit cards, put them in a clear plastic cup filled with water, and freeze them. Guess what happens? That's right—they're frozen! It's a nice visual and sends a clear message: DON'T USE ME! I told Rob and Marcia that story, and they did it.

Next I had them take three highlighters—say, green, yellow, and pink. (I call this the "Highlighter Exercise.") I told them to sit down together with their credit card statements and highlight in green all the purchases that were a "necessity." With the yellow marker I told them to highlight the ones they "liked to have" and with the pink mark the "nonessential and frivolous purchases." (An added benefit of the highlighter exercise is that it helps to identify any fraudulent purchases on your statement). For Rob and Marcia the results were eye opening. They never realized just how much money they were spending on happy hours, pricey lunches, costly cable TV service, and designer coffee.

From there we built a budget that included some fun money but also had them cut down on the unnecessary expenses. They began bringing lunch to work more often and limited the happy hours to fewer times per month. They bought Thermoses and filled them with fresh-brewed coffee from home. They got rid of HBO and Showtime in favor of Netflix, a bargain at a fraction of the price of cable. Together they set a feasible time period in which to get back to a zero balance and began having monthly financial dates to review their expenditures.

During this time Rob and Marcia were using just cash or pre-paid cards as methods of payment. Prepaid cards function exactly as credit cards do, except you can only spend what you have deposited and not a penny more. Consequently you're not racking up a balance that you can't pay off at the end of the month, which is a sound way to achieve financial stability.

Within two years Rob and Marcia slashed their debt from $15,000 down to $2,000, a much more manageable sum. Six years to create all that bad debt but only two years to whittle it down—not bad!

Rachel and Larry exemplify my **Phase Two: Bad Debt** clients. Larry, a dentist, and Rachel, a chiropractor, have two kids. Because both worked long hours, they felt guilty telling their children "no." Whenever the kids wanted a new toy or gadget, Larry and Rachel bought it for them, rationalizing it by telling themselves, "What's another $100 charge when it comes to our children's happiness?" They also had their kids enrolled in private school, with all the accompanying music and art lessons.

Eventually Rachel and Larry came to realize that they were in over their heads to the tune of $50,000 in credit card debt, but they didn't know how to stop. They knew they had a spending problem, but they couldn't help themselves. They didn't want to lose their social circle—dinners with friends, theater tickets, concerts, sporting events, shopping, golf dates—but they were spiraling down quickly, and the strain began taking a toll on their marriage.

Rachel and Larry were smart. They recognized they had a problem and were savvy enough to seek out an advisor to help them resolve it. They came to me willing to listen and wanting to get their financial house in order.

Because Rachel and Larry socialized in an upper-class community where they were constantly trying to keep up with the Joneses, the first thing I needed them to understand was that there was no shame in admitting they were making cutbacks to straighten out their finances. I explained to them that it's more humiliating to try to use a credit card and have it fail than it is to let friends know you're exercising some financial prudence. And you know what? There's a good chance the Joneses and perhaps even the Smiths are in the same financial boat as you are and just too embarrassed to admit it.

I also made it clear that they didn't have to become hermits just because they were tightening the purse strings. Why not entertain in their home? And if they absolutely had to try the hottest new restaurant in town, I told them to make a pact with each other that they wouldn't spend over a certain amount.

Keeping their kids in private school was a priority for them, so we had to figure out other ways to cut costs. This meant learning to say "no" to American Girl dolls, Legos, and stuff their kids "needed." I had them do the Highlighter Exercise to identify their various expenditures, paying special attention to the unnecessary and frivolous ones they should eliminate. Next I advised them to pay down their credit card debt one card at a time, starting with the smallest balance first.

This payment strategy makes a lot of sense psychologically. Here's why.

Say you have four credit cards, with $1,200, $3,000, $4,000, and $8,000 balances, respectively. Even if the $1,200 card has the lowest annual interest rate, you should pay that one off first. Although many people would suggest paying down the card with the highest interest rate, regardless of the balance owed, I disagree. I contend that people feel better—stronger, more in control—when they can eliminate an entire payment. In this case make the minimum payment on each of the four cards and put all additional funds toward the $1,200 debt. (Incidentally, any money that is not part of your customary income should be applied to paying off your debt, including raises and bonuses.) Tackling the smallest or most doable first creates a sense of accomplishment, a willingness to see it through.

Some people believe that transferring their balances to a card with a lower interest rate is a wise idea, and it can be, provided the new card has a *significantly* lower rate. If you can find one, then go for it. But beware! Though it sounds great, the fact is that you *are* opening up another credit card. You're feeding the credit beast! And the more credit cards you have open, the lower your credit score will likely fall because you're merely adding new debt. It's not the worst thing in the world, especially if you're on a greater mission to pay off that debt, yet it is something to consider. Ultimately Rachel and Larry decided against it. They simply did not want to open any more credit cards.

Larry and Rachel *did* vow to change their spending habits, which was a step in the right direction. I had them do an asset review, looking to identify items they could use to pay down their debt. (I've seen cases where people are $50,000 in debt, but they own thousands of dollars in assets). Finally, I told them to limit their credit cards to three. (We have an Amex, Visa, and Master-Card, and one that we keep in a safe at home just in case our wallets are stolen.) You don't need any more than that to run a household. Also, the more cards you have open, the greater the temptation to hide purchases.

Though they still owe money, Larry and Rachel managed to slash their credit card debt in half, down to $25,000 in three years. And guess what? Their kids have gotten along just fine without the latest and greatest from Mattel.

By the time you find yourself in **Phase Three: Terrible Debt**, you've all but reached the limit, like my clients Samantha and Eddie. They were only in their early thirties yet had amassed so much debt that they didn't know where to turn. Both were struggling actors living as if they were Angelina Jolie and Brad Pitt. They kept expecting to land that "big role" one day, but until that day came they were in crisis mode. Credit card companies called relentlessly, excoriating them for not paying their bills. Meanwhile the penalties continued to add up. The couple began dodging their friends and family because they were embarrassed about their finances. They tried repeatedly to get more credit cards, but—thankfully—they were turned down.

Sad to say, Samantha and Eddie were basically left with two choices: hire a debt consolidator or file for bankruptcy. An estimated 9 million Americans contact consumer credit counseling companies each year, so it's certainly a popular option. The debt consolidator acts as a negotiator between you and your credit card companies to whittle down your debt. For instance, rather than making five payments to five different credit card companies, you only make one payment to the consolidator, who spreads it out on your behalf.

It should be noted that this industry is riddled with fraud and preys upon desperate individuals. Many companies require a fee upfront. They make you sign a contract with heavy legal jargon and then they pick and choose the credit card companies with whom they want to work. If your credit card comes from a company they don't do business with, well, then, you're in the same situation you were at the beginning: a mess. Those card balances continue to go unpaid, your interest rates keep rising, and your debt continues to pile up.

At the end of the day debt consolidators are not doing anything you can't do yourself. Let me be blunt here: *you* got yourself into this mess, so *you* have to pick up the phone, call the credit card companies, and talk to them. Some will be willing to negotiate with you; others will not. No matter—it's worth a try. One couple I worked with cut their credit card interest rate in half simply by talking directly with the credit card company. Another got their rate down to 0 percent. Yes, you read that right: *zero, zilch, nada!* When it comes down to it, *you* are your own best advocate.

Bankruptcy is another course of action that can be taken to sort out overwhelming debt. (This necessitates hiring an attorney who specializes in bankruptcy law.) There are two main bankruptcy options: Chapter 7 and Chapter 13. In the case of Chapter 7 you are essentially starting over. With the exception of college loans, taxes, and child/spousal support, you wipe out your consumer debt. Car leases, mortgages, and creditors all go away, but so do the related assets. (If you do decide to keep the car or house or credit card, you are responsible for the overdue payments.) For those who file Chapter 7, the benefit comes in having a clean slate without the fear of being sued or having wages garnisheed or bank accounts levied.

According to Harlene Miller, a bankruptcy lawyer in Orange County, California, filing Chapter 7 *does* have its downside.[6] Bankruptcy results in a plummeting credit score, plus you will likely lose your existing credit cards. It's worth noting that even after you declare Chapter 7, you can still apply for credit cards. However, if they are offered, the interest rates will be exorbitantly high. Not to mention that you run the risk of piling up debt again, which defeats the purpose altogether.

Because having a credit card is a virtual necessity in today's world, if you file Chapter 7 and no one will offer you standard credit, what do you do? I recommend exploring a secured line of credit. I like to think of it as a credit card with training wheels: you make a deposit with the bank, which will then issue you the credit card. Your credit line is no larger than the initial bank deposit, and you cannot directly access the deposit with the bank. The cash acts as collateral for the card. This allows you to function in today's society while protecting you from racking up unsustainable debt again. Secured credit lines are also an excellent way to teach your college-age kids how to safely use credit cards.

Chapter 13 is another effective bankruptcy option. Here your debt is restructured for payment to creditors over a maximum five-year period. Your payment plan is based on income and necessary monthly living expenses. Any disposable income resulting from that budget is used to repay your debts. A Chapter 13 trustee approves your plan and facilitates the monthly payments. At that point all interest stops accruing on your credit card debt and the amount owed to each creditor becomes fixed. Chapter 13 is a good way to save your home when you have equity in it but can't make the current payments. Additionally, you'll get to keep any retirement and life insurance assets.

For Samantha and Eddie, Chapter 13 was the best option. Thankfully, they listened. We found them a bankruptcy lawyer to help them through the process. They will most likely be paying off their debt for the next five years, but at least they are on track.

Keep in mind that filing for bankruptcy is a life-changing decision. In exchange for the opportunity to wipe out or restructure your debt, you must often surrender your most prized possessions: your home, your car, your jewelry. Bankruptcy remains on your credit report for ten years, so your ability to obtain loans or even get a job in certain industries is compromised. Nonetheless, for those experiencing extreme financial duress, the upside of declaring bankruptcy can certainly outweigh the consequences of doing so. It is an opportunity for a "mulligan" or a "do over." Chapter 7, in particular, can only be filed once every ten years, so it's important to learn your lesson. Make a firm commitment to changing your spending habits en route to getting your financial plan back on track.

Phase Four: Deadly Debt is for all intents and purposes the breaking point, when all hope is lost. A few years ago I met with a woman named Evelyn, a forty-three-year-old, stay-at-home mom with two young children. She and her husband, Carl, had been married ten years. When I first spoke with Evelyn over the phone she was very interested in setting up a meeting. I suggested that she and Carl both attend, but she said that, because of his work schedule—Carl is a landscape designer—he couldn't make it. That's never a good sign. Experience has told me that when one person wants to show up alone, more often than not they're hiding something. But she was adamant about meeting, so we did.

As it turns out, Evelyn had amassed $65,000 in credit card debt, and because of the resulting high payments, she hadn't paid the mortgage on the family home in three months. She got herself into this predicament by way of poor money-management practices, like living beyond her means, and by monetarily supporting her parents who were struggling to make ends meet.

Not surprisingly, Evelyn was highly stressed about her family's financial situation. To make matters worse, she hadn't told Carl anything about their dire state of affairs, which only added to her anxiety (she handled all the money, so Carl had no clue they were sinking financially). She was desperate to dig out of the mess she was in. I explained to her that I could help but they would need to make sacrifices along with tough decisions regarding their finances. I also pointed out that she and Carl would only have success if they worked together.

I agreed to design a plan for them that would take steps toward improving their situation, but I told her I would do so only if both she and her husband came in to see me together. Knowing full well that their marriage would be tested when the truth came out, I suggested she consider talking to a marriage counselor before she spoke with Carl and before we all met to review their plan. She agreed, and we set a time to meet again in one month.

I called Evelyn a few days before our next scheduled meeting to confirm the appointment. She hadn't talked to a counselor nor had she come clean to Carl, but he'd found out anyway because the mortgage company had contacted him about the missed payments. At that point she confessed everything, and he was, to put it mildly, beside himself. Sadly, the marriage unraveled and our meeting never came to pass.

Their situation deeply upset me—it was so unnecessary and so avoidable. If Evelyn had only been upfront with Carl from the start, they would never have ended up in divorce court. Together they could have found a way out of the financial hole they were in *before* it swallowed up their marriage. It's precisely because of cases like this that I refer to the final phase of credit card debt as *deadly*. The crushing weight of their household debt effectively destroyed Evelyn and Carl's marriage. It transformed a once-healthy relationship into one devoid of communication, trust, and honesty, one that could not withstand life's financial hardships, self-inflicted or otherwise.

3

WHAT'S THE DIFFERENCE BETWEEN GOOD DEBT AND BAD DEBT?

I can't tell you how many people—good people, decent people—show up at my offices in terrible financial shape, all because of those small pieces of plastic called Visa, MasterCard, and American Express. And to make matters worse, many of these people, like Evelyn, keep their credit card woes a secret from their loved ones.

Let's not mince words: credit card debt is *bad* debt!

According to the Federal Reserve, Americans have $846.9 billion in credit card debt, or $15,112 per household.[7] Granted, that's down from more than $1 trillion in 2008, when the recession reached its peak, but it's still much more than we should owe.

As a January 2013 study in *Economic Inquiry* pointed out, many of those in debt are young people.[8] The report found that American credit card holders born between 1980 and 1984 have, on average, $5,689 more debt than their parents had at the same stage in their lives. According to researchers, they repay it more slowly and, thus, risk dying in debt if they don't curb their spending habits.

But that's unlikely to happen anytime soon. In the sixty years since their inception, credit cards have dramatically altered our purchasing behavior. They have changed our attitudes and feelings toward money and debt. Credit cards allow us to live beyond our means, making us think we're wealthier than we really are. This, in turn, causes us to spend money we don't have on items we don't need. Call me naive, but I sincerely doubt your life will be that much worse off with fewer pairs of fancy, high-end shoes in your closet. Since I'm a guy and you could make the argument that I just don't understand what it's like to be a woman, let me put it this way: none of us will suffer tremendously by not having the newest iWhatever or the latest and greatest golf clubs that claim to make your drive go five yards further (but alas, not straighter!).

Sure, many people have champagne tastes and beer budgets, but credit cards tend to make us forget about the Budweiser and go straight for the Dom Perignon. Because credit cards provide such easy access to capital, we forget it's merely a loan. It's fake money. Imagined money. *Money you don't have.*

According to a recent study, people spend 12 to 18 percent more when they swipe their cards than when they use cash.[9] Companies know this, which is why so many of them let customers use credit cards today. McDonald's, for example, found that its average transaction rose from $4.50 to $7.00 when customers were allowed to use credit cards to make their purchases rather than cash.

Credit cards have also encouraged laziness and a cavalier attitude toward debt. In the 1950s, for example, if you borrowed $200 from the bank to start a business and the business subsequently failed, you would have gotten a job and repaid that debt immediately. People took loans seriously; bankruptcy was considered disgraceful, so people borrowed much more carefully than they do today.

Not anymore! These days there's little stigma attached to debt. Because so many people have it, then it must be no big deal, something to make light of: "We're all in the same poverty-stricken boat together!"

Credit cards feed into our national need for immediate gratification, adding even more fire to the YOLO generation. I'm all for seizing the moment and embracing the *now*, but not when it involves blind spending and a wild lack of self-control. And that's exactly what credit cards do: they zero in on people with major impulse-control problems, only intensifying addictive personalities.

Like drug, alcohol, gambling, or food addictions, credit cards can provide a false sense of euphoria. This is no great shock: credit card companies deliberately hook you, the trusting consumer. They know what they're doing—enticing you with a million frequent flier miles, 0 percent interest rates, or free gifts for a certain number of dollars spent.

They're brilliant marketers with ingenious ways of reeling you in. It can be very alluring until you get slammed with a mammoth bill and minimum payments that are impossible to repay.

And when that happens those friendly credit cards folks, who were so deferential when you first signed up, will suddenly change their tune. They have tremendous resources at their disposal to collect the money owed them, and they will use the full weight of those resources to make your life miserable: relentless phone calls, skyrocketing interest rates, a damaging credit score, and so on.

Good luck getting another card or buying a house or car in the near future!

It's easy to put your head in the sand and say, "It'll all work out!" And it might—you never know. Maybe you'll hit the lottery. But more than likely you won't, and you'll spend the rest of your days trying to dig yourself out of a very unpleasant financial hole.

Want me to stop?

I will.

But indulge me for one more minute.

Credit card debt doesn't just affect your finances. People with credit card debt tend to shirk on their health too, as a study by sociologists at the University of Michigan found. According to the study, published in the April 2013 *Journal of Health and Social Behavior*, more than 64 percent of those who were ill but hadn't seen a doctor said they were indebted to credit card companies and couldn't afford medical care.[10]

Debt has a negative impact on your relationship too. A January 2013 survey of 1,005 adults conducted by CreditCards.com reported that 53 percent of Americans polled consider heavy debt a major turnoff in a relationship.[11] Roughly three in five Americans—62 percent of women and 53 percent of men—said they would have less trust in a prospective partner who was in serious debt. Finding out that a significant other kept big credit card debt a secret or lied about his or her finances was enough to kill the relationship.

Phew.

Now that I've gotten that off my chest, I want you to know that I do live in the real world. I know you're not going to stop using credit cards—heck, *I* use credit cards. They're easy, they're convenient, and I like those same perks I was maligning just a few paragraphs earlier.

What's more, they're a *necessity* in today's world. Ever try to book a hotel without a credit card? Or purchase an airline ticket? Or rent a car? Or shop online? That's right. Unthinkable. And nearly impossible.

I am, however, fundamentally opposed to using credit cards as a tool to live beyond your means. In our household we pay off our credit cards every month, compulsively. Now, for those of you who were confounded earlier when I said that my brother-in-law, a police detective, advises against using debit cards *at all*, here's a simple solution to the question, "Really Jeff, no debit cards? You clearly dislike credit cards, so now what?!" First of all, I want you to think of a credit card more as a form of payment and less as a pot of spending money. Use it as you would a check or debit card, which are only good if you have sufficient funds to back them. Treat your credit card like a debit card by charging only up to the amount you can afford to pay off each month. Nowadays it's easy to track your spending online or with a simple phone call. Otherwise, like most Americans, you'll find yourself using your credit card to spend money you don't have, resulting in an accumulation of bad debt that you certainly don't need.

Look at it this way: say you decide to bust out the Amex card and drop $500 on that top-of-line TaylorMade driver you've been eyeing for weeks. If you then elect to make only the minimum payment on that card each month, assuming a 19 percent interest rate, by the time you pay off that balance your new golf club just cost you a whopping $998. That's twice the price! You don't need to be an economics whiz to recognize that's just dumb.

WHAT ABOUT LOANING MONEY TO FRIENDS AND FAMILY?

Loans to friends or family members can be very bad, but they don't have to be: you just have to be smart about it.

If you do loan out money, you must treat the transaction as a business deal, complete with a formal contract in place. Whether it's your closest friend or your wife's sister, you must draw up a document outlining how much is owed, when it must be repaid, and how much interest you are (or aren't) charging. This creates accountability and increases the likelihood that you'll actually get paid back.

My clients, Glen and Judith, loaned their fifty-year-old daughter, Maggie, almost $50,000 so she could put a down payment on a new house. Glen and Judith insisted that their lawyer write up a plan, and Maggie wholeheartedly agreed. They mapped out the terms, and Maggie paid her parents back within the committed time frame.

Clearly $50,000 is a large chunk of change. But it doesn't matter how big or small the sum: you don't loan out money without protecting yourself, even if it's your own kid. If you don't feel comfortable making it legal, then you might as well just give it away as a gift. When you loan someone money with the expectation of being paid back, you *must* have an agreement in place. Without one you're setting yourself up for a lot of potential trouble down the road. Friendships end and family feuds begin all on account of well-intentioned loans that go unrecovered. Thanksgiving dinner is never quite the same when all you have to be thankful for is the fact that you have somehow managed to refrain from dropping the bowl of sweet potatoes in the lap of your no-good brother-in-law who still owes you a vacation's worth—or two!—of cash. And, for the sake of your marriage, make certain that you as a couple have fully discussed and agreed to make the loan *together*. Without the consent of both partners, I would strongly advise against it.

SHOULD WE CONTINUALLY REFINANCE OUR HOME?

Your primary residence is not an investment—it's your home, the roof under which you live, the place where you will raise your family. It should *not* be used as an ATM!

People typically refinance their home to lower their monthly payments (potentially a good move) or to put cash in their pockets by pulling out equity (potentially a bad move). When you take out a chunk of money—that is, use your home as an ATM—and then spend it frivolously, you are simply increasing your home's debt burden. Although many people *say* they're going to use that money to fix up the house, which can improve its value, or to pay off some old bills, which reduces bad debt, more often than not they spend it on a lavish vacation or on a new car, which accomplishes neither.

Refinancing is a tricky business. In theory you can keep refinancing your home as many times as you want for the rest of your life. Sounds swell, but keep in mind that each time you refinance into a new thirty-year loan, the clock resets on your thirty years of payments, so your chances of ever reaching the finish line—owning your home outright—are slim because you keep getting sent back to the starting gate. To make matters worse, habitual refinancing gives rise to additional payments later on in life. These outlays could delay your plans to retire comfortably by forcing you to work longer than you'd anticipated.

Caveat: If interest rates drop so much that you can lower your payments and keep your same terms (i.e., the number of years you'll be paying on the loan), then I'm not opposed to refinancing under those circumstances.

If you *do* refinance with the intent of taking equity out of your home, make sure you do so for a specific purpose, like taking care of serious credit card debt. The idea is to eradicate your bad debt, leaving you only owing money on your real estate. Refinancing can be an effective tool for achieving this goal; however, merely racking up more credit card balances by continuing to live beyond your means negates any gains made.

WHAT ABOUT OUR STUDENT LOAN DEBT?

On the whole, student loans should not be considered bad debt. Why? The interest rates tend to be relatively low by comparison. Besides, when you decided to take one out, you did so to further your education. Studies show that individuals who get a degree have a higher earning potential over their lifetime than those who do not. So it's an investment in yourself. That being said, I will touch on student loans in the context of whether you are getting a solid return on your investment when we get to the chapter on college planning.

But if you are a couple who already has student loan debt, then it needs to be part of your monthly budget expenses. You must pay it off, so make it part of your plan. If you want to accelerate the payments or, better yet, are in a position to pay it off early, by all means, go for it! The idea here is simple: the faster you can eliminate your debt—good, bad, or otherwise—the further along you'll be on the path to financial freedom.

4

HOW DO WE ALIGN OUR GOALS AND EXPECTATIONS?

A carefully crafted game plan is your ticket to financial independence, but only if you and your spouse are both working together to realize your shared vision for the future. You might be thinking, "Okay Jeff, we've got our plan, but how do we stick to it without sticking it to each other in the process?" While there is no magic formula for success, it's been my experience that couples who stay the course have a few things in common: they've aligned their goals, and they regularly communicate their expectations on how to reach them.

When I talk with most couples about their primary goals—those biggies we mentioned earlier, such as house buying, college savings, or retirement planning—they're usually in sync. How they prioritize them may differ, but any ensuing disagreements are usually fairly tame.

The more heated disputes tend to arise when it comes to funding these goals and other expenditures. Sometimes there just aren't enough dollars in the checking account at the end of the month to fund everything to everyone's satisfaction. Other times there might be extra funds lying around but you're at odds over where to direct them. If you find yourselves bickering about priorities, then you need to sort through it all and find some common ground—perfect Financial Date Night fodder! In most cases the real solution can be found by reevaluating your lifestyle spending.

This is the area where a disconnect often occurs—for example, she wants to invest money on new carpeting for the home, whereas he would rather spend it on a Caribbean cruise. In other cases couples are simply oblivious to each other's spending habits. How much did those new golf clubs cost anyway? What is a reasonable amount to spend each month on new clothes?

What's more, how do you feel about spending on luxuries, and how, exactly, do you define "luxuries"? If your definition of luxury is a night at the Ritz Carlton and your partner's is a movie and the all-you-can-eat special at Red Lobster, chances are you have different definitions of *luxury*. Likewise, if you have your heart set on driving a new BMW every three years and your spouse views this as a complete waste of money, well, then, you guessed it! You don't see eye to eye in this department.

That's okay. It doesn't mean you're doomed for divorce, but it *does* mean you have to figure out what things you like individually, what things you enjoy together, and what things are the absolute non-negotiables. Getting them all on the table is the first step toward reaching a mutual understanding and keeping your game plan on track.

Let's begin with me. I absolutely *love* coffee. ("Hi, I'm Jeff, and I'm a coffee-aholic!"). I love a big, fat cup o' joe. I love everything about it—the taste, the smell, the ritual of making and drinking it. I am, I confess, a bit of a coffee snob—Folger's simply won't suffice.

Kendra, however, doesn't drink coffee at all. It's something she never took a liking to and, therefore, would never choose to spend money on. If she were to say to me, "Jeff, I love you, but we're on a budget and you've got to cut the coffee habit," I assure you the withdrawals would begin at the mere thought of it!

And then I'd get to thinking: if I couldn't buy my highbrow brew, what would I do? Realistically, if I lost my job and had no income, I'd need to adjust. But, apart from incurring a financial calamity in which mutual sacrifices must be made, if you've got a plan and you're putting money away as I suggest, there should be room in the budget for those things that give you joy (e.g., java!). Reasonable, individual expenditures should not need to be sacrificed just because they're not a priority for your spouse. Acknowledge them, accept them, account for them—your relationship will be better off for it.

Then there are things you enjoy as a couple, such as attending the theater, antiquing, sporting events, ballroom dancing, to name just a few. Take my in-laws for example: each fall they buy season tickets to go watch their favorite college football team play. They attend all the home games and, on occasion, will even follow the team to other campuses across the country. It's something they love to do; it's a passion of theirs, so they willingly allocate funds toward it.

Kendra and I share a passion for wine. We both like to drink a good, full-bodied bottle and aren't afraid to drop $60 on one, especially over an expensive meal. We probably spend about $600 or more a month on wine (that's factoring in dinners plus wine, once or twice a week). That's over $7,000 annually on wine and dinners alone.

Now, you could argue that this is a luxury—drinking a cool, refreshing glass of the house tap water would certainly put more cash in our pockets. But two things are at play here. First, based on our income, that expense is within our budget. And second, we consider our mutual interest in wine a *priority*—it's something we share together that's ours. No one's compromising here. We deem it money well spent for the value and enjoyment we derive from it.

And still, even though we can afford it, we keep ourselves in check. Kendra and I still live in the same suburban, middle-income home we bought twenty years ago; we owe less than $100,000 on it. Yeah, sometimes I think it would be nice to own a place by the beach. But residing where we do gives us a lot more discretionary income than we would have if we lived in a beachfront, seven-figure home. Yes, we could swing it. But if we did, we'd probably have at least a $7,000 monthly mortgage payment, which would last twenty years, easily. Bye-bye wine allowance! Why on earth would we want to subject ourselves to that?

As far as Kendra and I are concerned, our annual family vacation to Hawaii is an absolute non-negotiable expense, but one that is hardly cheap. While we're not staying at the Four Seasons, we're not exactly holed up at the Oahu Motel 6 either. Again, this is a *shared luxury*, something we do as a family. We make it a priority. We plan for it. We look forward to it. We would be terribly disappointed if we had to forgo it.

Having said all that, I want you to know that I shop for clothes on an as-needed basis. As the president of my firm, it's important that I look put together, and I wear my share of high-end brands. My suits look great, they're impeccably made, but I buy them at Nordstrom Rack for $600 rather than $1,200 at a department store. I'm not a thrift store shopper, but Kendra likes Marshall's and TJ Maxx, especially for the kids, when they're growing so quickly. Why pay all that money for clothing they'll likely outgrow within a year, if not months?

Obviously, we all have different incomes and budgets, so what may seem like a luxury to me might be a drop in the bucket to you. Conversely, if you're earning $80,000 as a couple, then the things I'm talking about are off your radar. But it's important to continuously ask yourselves: Is this a realistic purchase within our budget? You'll find that what's out of reach for now might not be in a year or so.

And though your incomes, your priorities, and even your shared interests may change over time, some fundamental principles should always remain, like living within your means, paying yourself first, and keeping honest and open communications with your spouse. These are the hallmark of any effective financial game plan.

5

INVESTING 101: WHERE DO WE INVEST OUR GAME PLAN?

Once you have your game plan in place, one in which you and your spouse are ready, willing, and able to follow, then it's time to talk investing. If you immediately start thinking bulls and bears, stocks and bonds, buy low sell high, then I implore you to STOP. Many people mistakenly view investing as a way to get rich quick. On the contrary, when you connect it to a set of goals, investing takes on a whole new meaning; think of it as the vehicle (or risk level) wherein you put your hard-earned money that funds the rooms (goals) of your financial house. Investing is not about trying to make a million dollars overnight. If that's your mindset, head to Vegas. And good luck—you'll need it.

When it comes to investing it's really about picking the *appropriate* investment vehicle to get you to your destination. How far you have to go (your goal) and how much time you have to get there will determine the most suitable vehicle (risk level). Distance and time matter. If, for example, you are planning a trip across the country—retirement goal—there are a variety of ways to get there: you could drive a car, fly on an airplane, take the train, ride the bus, or even ride a bike. Factoring in the amount of time you have will rule out some of these options en route to determining which one is the best fit.

Before we start talking strategy or begin looking at some of the different investment options, let's do a quick run-through to be sure you have your financial house in order.

Have you created a budget (land/foundation/flooring)? How will you know how much you can invest if you don't know how much you can consistently save? I've met with couples who have investment portfolios and savings plans yet have no budget. I'll ask them how much they can save on a monthly basis, and they both look at me, then back at each other, then back at me—they have no idea. They put money away on occasion—which is good, don't get me wrong—but a budget gives you the ability to a look at the whole financial picture and gauge where additional savings dollars can be found.

Have you eliminated any bad debt? Most of your revolving debt (i.e., credit card debt) carries double-digit interest rates, some over 20 percent. It's ridiculous to begin investing if you are carrying a credit card balance at these astronomical rates. No matter the investment vehicles you choose, they're not going to bring you those types of after-tax investment returns. Invest in paying off your bad debt first before investing in the market. If someone tells you they can get you consistent investment returns that will beat your credit card interest rate charges, then they also have a bridge from California to Hawaii to sell you—that's not the person you want helping you with your investment decisions.

Do you have a solid 911 Fund (walls)? Investing involves layers of risk. Before you can think about putting dollars into vehicles that fluctuate, you need to have a stable financial house with solid walls. If the washing machine breaks down and needs replacing, you don't want to tap your investment accounts to buy a new one. What if the investment you purchased is at an all-time low, yet you need the money ASAP? Those are expenses that your 911 Fund should cover.

WHAT DO WE NEED TO DISCUSS AS A COUPLE BEFORE WE BEGIN INVESTING?

"Okay, Jeff, our financial house is in order. We have a nice piece of land, a solid foundation with good flooring, some sturdy walls, zero bad debt, and we have some money left over each month to invest in our game plan. Now what?"

An excellent question, my friends.

During one of your Financial Date Nights spend some time prioritizing your goals. If you are eager to buy a house or upgrade your existing one and you're both in agreement as to its urgency, then put that goal at the top of the list. Maybe you have a couple of kids who you'd like to see graduate from college, so make that a high priority. I can't tell you which one to put ahead of another—your goals are your own. But I *can* offer you some friendly advice: it would be foolhardy to relegate your retirement goal to the bottom spot on your list. We're talking about your financial independence here, the day work becomes an option. Stay mindful of its importance in your overall game plan.

But let's take a look at what happens if my retirement advice falls on deaf ears and you decide to put off saving for another five or even ten years.

Meet the Dewers and the Laggers, two couples who share the same age but not the same investment priorities. The Dewers were twenty-five years old when they started saving $2,000 annually for retirement, but they stopped at age thirty-three. During those eight years their contributions totaled $16,000.

A CASE FOR STARTING EARLY

Age	Dewers' contributions	Laggers' contributions
25	$2,000	$0
26	2,000	0
27	2,000	0
28	2,000	0
29	2,000	0
30	2,000	0
31	2,000	0
32	2,000	0
33	0	2,000
34	0	2,000
35	0	2,000
36	0	2,000
37	0	2,000
38	0	2,000
39	0	2,000
40	0	2,000
41	0	2,000
42	0	2,000
43	0	2,000
44	0	2,000
45	0	2,000
46	0	2,000
47	0	2,000
48	0	2,000
49	0	2,000
50	0	2,000
51	0	2,000
52	0	2,000
53	0	2,000
54	0	2,000
55	0	2,000
56	0	2,000
57	0	2,000
58	0	2,000
59	0	2,000
60	0	2,000
Total contribution	$16,000	$56,000
Total value at 10% per year	$362,817	$295,262

Source: Trilogy Financial training chart.

The Laggers took a different approach. Instead of starting right away, they waited until age thirty-three to begin saving for retirement, investing $2,000 every year up to age sixty. The Laggers contributed a total of $56,000 over that time period. Assuming both accounts earned the same interest rate, who do you think accumulated more retirement money by the time they turned sixty— the Dewers or the Laggers? Let's find out.

As you can see from the table, the Dewers' account is, in fact, worth more than the Laggers'. That's $67,555 additional dollars that the Dewers get to spend in their golden years. The Laggers invested $40,000 *more* yet wound up with *less*. How can that be, you ask? It's the power of starting early coupled with the power of compound interest—very powerful indeed!

Let's take it even a step further.

What if the Dewers kept *doing*? In other words, what if they continued investing $2,000 a year until age sixty rather than stopping at thirty-two? Well, their account balance would have been $701,098. Not too shabby. This story clearly illustrates the impact *time* has on investing, how it can work for or against you. The choice is yours, but as you can plainly see, the earlier you start, the better off you'll be. Just ask the Dewers!

HOW MUCH SHOULD WE INVEST TO START?

Because we're talking about investing in your primary goals (rooms), the objective, as you may recall, is 15 percent or more of your gross income (before taxes)—the *pay yourself first* principle. If you've been living paycheck to paycheck, this may seem like a monumental task. But reviewing your budget and getting your priorities straight will help you make headway on increasing your savings rate. And although 15 percent is the target, you can certainly start with less. Some investments will allow you to put away as little as $25 on a monthly basis. The aim here, above all others—as the Dewers demonstrated—is to just *start*!

BUT JEFF, WHERE DO WE START?

Start with learning. One of the most important rules to remember about investing is "understanding what you own and why you own it." You'll sleep better at night for it. The more knowledgeable you are about your investments, the less likely you are to let feelings get in the way of your common sense, which often results in irrational decision making. We are all well aware that trying to make decisions with emotions running high usually leads to one of two things: poor decisions or heated arguments . . . and, many times, both! A real losing combination.

I always tell clients it's my job to take their emotions out of investing and keep their heads focused on the big picture. By understanding what they own, this becomes far simpler to achieve.

So let's start by getting acquainted with some investment fundamentals. The basics. Everything you need to know but might be afraid to ask.

WHAT IS A STOCK?

Stocks (a.k.a. equities) represent ownership in a business. When you buy a share of stock in a company, you become an owner. Stocks function to make their owner money in two primary ways. The first is by appreciating in price. If, for example, you bought a share of Google stock for $75 two years ago and today it's selling for $80 a share, then the value of your investment has gone up. You are buying the stock with the expectation that the share price will increase over time. This is affectionately referred to as "buy low, sell high."

The second way you make money in stocks is through dividends. A dividend is essentially your portion of the company's profits. Most dividends are paid in cash, but some are issued to shareholders in additional stock. The company's board of directors decides whether a dividend will be paid. By the way, when you own a share of stock you get to vote on who those directors are. Talk about perks!

So to sum it up, there are two main ways to make money in individual stocks: through price appreciation and through dividends. Sounds good, you might say, and because we're coffee-aholics like you, Jeff, we want to be owners in Starbucks, so put all our retirement savings into shares of Starbucks straight away!

Whoa, not so fast, coffee kin!

I must forewarn you of the pitfalls of stocks, particularly single-issued stock investments. To start with, not all companies pay dividends, and those that do certainly aren't guaranteed—they're issued based on the overall performance of the company. Next, stocks don't always go up in value, especially in the short term. If the stock price falls and you need to sell, you'll have lost some of your investment. If the company goes out of business, well, as you probably guessed, your investment goes out of business too. Your retirement savings is simply too important to throw it all into a vehicle of that risk level.

There are intelligent ways to participate in stocks, and I will get to that momentarily, but let's discuss bonds first.

WHAT IS A BOND?

Bonds (a.k.a. debt) are loans. When you purchase a bond you are loaning your money to an entity. Corporations and governments are the largest issuers of bonds. Why do they sell bonds to investors? For several reasons. Maybe a company wants to expand its business or a county wants to build some new infrastructure (e.g., a bridge or sewer plant). In exchange for loaning your money in the form of a bond, you are entitled to a few guarantees. First, the corporation or government guarantees your principal—that is, they promise to pay you back the amount you loaned them. Second, you are guaranteed an interest rate (a.k.a. coupon or yield) on the bond.

But although bonds do offer guarantees, *the guarantee is only as good as the guarantor*. If the company you loan your money to does not perform well, then how are they going to pay you your interest? Even worse: if they go under and default on their debt (same as defaulting on a house loan), then you might not get all or any of your loan back.

As with stocks, there are many different types of bonds you can purchase.

Much like individual households, corporations and governments have a credit rating too (think of it as their FICO score). The higher the credit rating, the better their guarantee. A higher credit rating also means they can offer a lower interest rate to bondholders. Conversely, a bond with a higher interest rate will yield more monthly income, but that comes with a higher risk of the issuer defaulting on the bond.

Bonds that offer really high interest rates are commonly known as "junk" bonds. At the other end of the bond spectrum are US government bonds, or treasuries. These are backed by the "full faith and credit" of the US government. In return for that high degree of safety you get—drum roll please—a low interest rate!

Another type of government bond is a municipal bond, or "muni." States, counties, and other municipalities issue these bonds. A nice "muni" perk is that the interest the investor earns is federally tax-free; however, municipal bonds offer fewer guarantees than US treasuries.

Now that you have a better understanding of stock and bond basics, I want to teach you a simple investment approach that can help you build wealth and ultimately reach your goals—investing in stocks and bonds through mutual funds or exchange traded funds (ETFs).

Let's talk about mutual funds first.

Mutual funds are simply a pooling of investor dollars—in this case yours—with a common objective. While stock mutual funds aim for growth, bond mutual funds offer income and safety. Still others have a blend of both stocks and bonds (a.k.a. hybrid or balanced funds). The stocks provide the growth, whereas the bonds provide the safety of principal. If you think of it like driving your car, the stocks are the accelerator and the bonds are the brake.

Mutual funds have gained in popularity over the last few decades, becoming a $15 trillion industry. They have effectively moved Wall Street to Main Street, giving middle-America access to the same portfolio managers the uber-wealthy have used for generations. Some of the benefits they offer include:

Professional management (a.k.a. portfolio manager): Mutual fund companies hire full-time portfolio managers. Their job is to pick what securities (stocks or bonds) to own. The portfolio manager's sole objective is to get the highest rate of return while staying within the stated objectives of the fund.

If the mutual fund objective is growth, then the portfolio manager's job is to research and pick stocks with a high growth potential. On the flipside, if the fund aims to provide a monthly income and safety of principal, the fund manager will look for bonds that meet those criteria.

Diversification: Unlike investing in a single company stock or bond (*no* diversification), a mutual fund allows you to invest in a *large basket* of stocks and/or bonds (usually over one hundred); this diversifies your risk over a greater number of companies. So I ask you: if you were investing your retirement savings, would you rather put your money in one company or one hundred different companies? Before you answer that, what if you pick one company and it goes out of business prior to your retirement? Your entire investment would be gone. Now, what if you pick one hundred companies and one goes belly up? That's right, the ninety-nine other companies are still in business. That's why diversification matters.

Flexibility and low minimums: Mutual funds are easy to set up, and as I mentioned earlier, some even allow you to invest as little as $25 a month. That $25 hires the same professional management and benefits from the same diversification as someone who invests $100,000. Although that investor owns more shares of the fund, you both get identical service and investment performance. Incidentally, mutual funds do go up and down in value. A monthly or quarterly statement details the number of shares you own and your current account balance. Mutual funds are also very liquid investment vehicles, which means they are easy to sell quickly if need be.

Let's move on to exchange traded funds, or ETFs.

The last decade has seen ETFs explode in popularity. They are similar to mutual funds in that they are a pooling of investment—your—dollars with a common objective. An ETF's objective (goal) is to mimic the index it is benchmarking. Now, before you tune out, stick with me here.

You've likely at least heard of the more popular indexes—Standard & Poor's (S&P), Dow Jones, the NASDAQ. The media frequently report on these indexes. When you hear, "The S&P climbed fifty points this week" or "The Dow Jones was down for the day," that means your investments went up or down accordingly.

For example, assume you wanted to invest part of your retirement savings in the S&P index, so you purchase an ETF that mirrors the performance of the S&P. Let's say the S&P index had a pretty good year and was up 8 percent. Your S&P ETF account would also be up 8 percent, minus any fees . . . ah yes, let's talk costs for a minute.

One of the perceived advantages of an ETF over a mutual fund is the typically lower annual management fee charged to you, the investor. While most mutual funds are actively managed by a portfolio manager, ETFs use a passive management process, often derived from a computer-generated algorithm that lowers their costs.

ETFs are bought and sold during trading hours like stocks, whereas mutual fund share prices are determined at the end of every trading day. Like mutual funds, there are a great many ETF investment options available.

Before you jump into buying a mutual fund or ETF, do your homework. There are loads of websites to turn to for information. But buyer beware: many of those sites are trying to *sell* you something. Make sure you understand what you are purchasing before you click.

A simple way to invest in ETFs or mutual funds is by using a technique called dollar cost averaging (DCA). Dollar cost averaging is a convenient way to invest a specific dollar amount on a monthly basis. One of the benefits of DCA is that over time you have the potential to lower your average cost per share.

Let's work through an example.

Imagine that in a year's time you invested $1,000 a month into Fund A. In January the price per share was $10, and by December it increased to $20. During that twelve-month period you would have purchased 835.44 shares at an average cost per share of $14.38, for an account value totaling $16,708.

Now let's take a look at a different scenario with that same $1,000 per month. Say you purchased an investment in Fund B that started at $10 per share, but the share price declined over the first six months then climbed back to $10 a share again by the year's

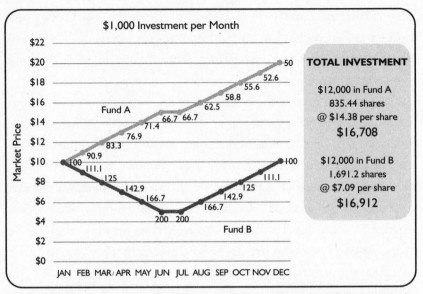

*This is a hypothetical example that reflects no particular investment and is for illustration purposes only. Dollar cost averaging does not assure a profit or protect against losses. Such a plan involves continuous investments in securities regardless of fluctuating price levels of such securities and the investor should consider his/her financial ability to continue purchases through periods of low levels.

end. Under these conditions you were able to buy more shares at a lower price per share, resulting in an account value of $16,912.

Although this is not always the case, in this example over a twelve-month period dollar cost averaging into a "fluctuating fund" actually made you more money than investing into a fund that continually increased over the same period.

Dollar cost averaging can help mitigate the effects of market volatility, but it does not altogether eliminate the R word—*risk*. Risk is a funny word. When I ask couples to define it, I get some mighty interesting responses, ranging from, "I don't want to lose a dime of my hard-earned money" to "I'm good with taking huge risks so I can become a millionaire next week!"

Everyone has a different risk tolerance, but there's one simple standard of measurement that I like most: the Sleep Test. I tell clients that taking a risk should never keep you or your spouse up at night. If you're losing sleep over a particular aspect of your plan, then it's time to scale it back or obtain more clarity.

Investments and risk go hand in hand. Remember, the first rule of investing is "Understand what you own and why you own it." If it's too complicated or doesn't make any sense to you, then stay away.

The second rule of investing is "If it's sounds too good to be true, then it probably is." Steer clear of the "can't lose" or "instant big money" scene. I tell prospective clients that if they're looking for someone to make them a millionaire overnight, then they've knocked on the wrong door. I'm a create-a-plan-and-stick-to-it-and-watch-it-grow-over-the-long-haul kinda guy.

IT'S ABOUT TIME, NOT TIMING

Attempting to time the market—taking all your money out of the market and putting it in a bank, then reinvesting it when the "time is right"—is a super strategy *if* you have a crystal ball and can see into the future. Otherwise it's a foolish proposition—market timers have to be right *twice*: once when they take money out and then again when they put it back in.

I hearken back to 2008, arguably the worst recession and largest stock market drop in my lifetime, to validate my point. During those angst-filled weeks and months we advised clients to stay mindful of their goals and objectives, to sit tight, and to not let their frayed nerves unduly influence their game plans. For many, retirement was still ten, twenty, or even thirty years out in the future. We encouraged them to remain disciplined and keep their emotions in check.

Granted, that's extremely difficult to do when every newspaper, magazine, TV show, and website inundates us with downright dismal news and numbers. It's even harder when, as part of a couple, you invariably have one spouse who is much more risk averse than the other. In this case communication becomes paramount.

I understand the desire by one or both of you to pull all of your money out of the market and put it in a bank account or money market fund; after all, nobody likes to see the account values on their statements go in reverse. In 2007 the Dow Jones was over 14,000, and everyone enjoyed opening the mail! In 2008 all hell broke loose. If, after the Dow dropped below 7,000, you reacted by moving your money completely out of the market and into cash, the next time you opened your statement your account value was roughly 50 percent less. (That's when people began calling their 401(k) statements their 201(k)!)

A couple I recently met, the Hendersons, were not clients of ours back in 2008, but I sure wish they had been. They were in their late fifties then and, after years of work, had amassed about a million dollars in their 401(k) plan, with 100 percent of it invested in the stock market (mistake number one). The 2008 market correction hit, and that million dollars became about $500,000 in the blink of an eye. Talk about scary! They lost half of their purchasing power. Panicked, they whisked it out of the market and put it into a savings account at their local bank, which paid little to no interest (mistake number two). Had they been able to weather the storm, the market has since rebounded, and today they'd be right back at that million-dollar mark—and then some.

Surely there will be more corrections/recessions in the future— it's the cyclical nature of the market—so it's critical to keep the lines of communication open and your emotions under control. It is equally important to stay mindful of your investment timelines as you work toward achieving your financial goals. For instance, it's unwise to be fully invested in the stock market with a retirement horizon of a year or less. On the flipside, a thirty-something couple with $75,000 in a retirement account should not be concerned about short-term market swings but instead should remain focused on their long-term growth opportunities.

Incidentally, short-term investments are also about goal planning. Let's say you're newly married and are saving for a house. Most people are excited and wish they could buy one "tomorrow." But in most cases tomorrow is not realistic. Your time frame must be in years, not days. A better vehicle for this money would be one with low volatility and less risk. Why? Because two years from now you don't want Wall Street to correct once again, along with your hard-earned cash. Then you'll have to put off purchasing your house until the market rebounds.

WHEN IT COMES TO INVESTING, MAKE TIME YOUR FRIEND, NOT YOUR ENEMY

By investing early, time becomes your friend, as it did for the Dewers. In the same vein, procrastinating, like the Laggers, turns time against you. Procrastination, as I see it, is short-term pleasure with long-term pain: more spending money in your pocket today—whoopee!—working into your seventies because you can't afford not to—ouch.

So the earlier you start saving, the more time works in your favor—doing so increases the time frame in which you have to reach your objective (and to take advantage of the power of compound interest). With that being said, just because you didn't or can't start investing early doesn't mean you are doomed for the poorhouse. As beneficial as that element is, it's perhaps more imperative that, given your time frame (goal), you choose the appropriate investment vehicle (risk level). Time becomes your enemy when the investment vehicle is ill suited for the time frame. Remember, the longer your time frame, the more risk you can assume as a couple.

Let's take a look at some examples.

"We want to buy a house in the next three years." Is this a short-term goal that warrants less risk? If you said yes, then you are correct.

"We have a seven-year-old and want to start socking away money for college. What's our time frame?" Unless you have a little Einstein under your roof, you have roughly ten years before it comes time to write that first college tuition check. Can you handle more risk and fluctuation than our house-saving example above? You bet.

"We are twenty-five years old and want to start saving for retirement—financial independence. How much risk can we assume?" With a time frame of thirty to forty years you can certainly push the risk envelope, so long as it passes the Sleep Test.

Congratulations, you have officially completed Jeff's Investing 101! Use the knowledge you've gained and apply it to your financial house, staying mindful of the fact that investing is a serious business that requires serious thought and understanding. This is not fun money we are talking about; make sure you and your spouse are both in agreement before diving into a particular investment. If you are having any reservations whatsoever, consult with a professional (I will cover how to find a good one in Chapter 18). A solid investment advisor will put a plan together and walk you through the entire process, putting both your minds at ease so you can proceed down the investment path with confidence.

6

SHOULD WE BUY LIFE INSURANCE?

Life insurance (roof) serves a dual purpose for couples. It can be used to satisfy any debt obligations (e.g., mortgage loan) and it can be used to replace lost income from the unfortunate death of a spouse. Replacing that lost income is crucial in helping keep your financial house in order.

If you have dependent children, you absolutely need a life insurance policy. If something were to happen to you, your family must be properly taken care of so as not to suffer financially. You have a moral obligation to not leave a financial burden on your family.

Furthermore, if you purchase a home, you then have a joint financial interest that needs to be satisfied should one of you die.

When you get married, you vow to take care of the other person for richer or poorer, for better or worse. If you're both working and one of you were to die suddenly, would the other person be able to survive without your income? Yes or no? In today's society too often the answer is no!

What if the surviving spouse could manage financially, but the grieving period was so challenging for them that they couldn't go back to work right away? Or what if there are children involved who might need extra help coping with the loss of a parent? My office has seen several cases in which young and presumably healthy clients get diagnosed with a terminal or debilitating disease, the most common being cancer. Almost everyone knows a close friend or family member who's been stricken by this horrible disease. Many times having life insurance coverage is the only bright news in an otherwise very bleak situation.

In some instances these clients beat the odds and were eventually cured. The key word here is *eventually*. Thanks to having properly structured life insurance contracts in place, we were able to "tap" into their death benefit to pay their bills. Imagine that: life insurance you don't have to die to use! These policies have what we refer to as accelerated benefits riders (ABRs). They are part of our normal planning process, the roof of your financial house.

Take me, for example. If I were to die without having set up a mechanism to replace the income I make, then I'd be shirking the moral obligation I have to provide for the well-being of my family. By the same token, even though my wife does not contribute to the household income, she does play an invaluable role in our family by staying at home every day raising our two children. If she were to die, there would be a dramatic change in our household, and some of the challenges would be financial. Who would be there for our kids day in and day out? Would I need to pay for someone to care for them while I worked? What about taking care of the house? Although life insurance does not necessarily solve all these problems, it certainly helps deal with them from a financial standpoint.

WHAT TYPE OF LIFE INSURANCE IS BEST FOR US?

Properly designed life insurance covers several potential risks:

1. Life
2. Disability

3. Long-term care
4. Terminal or critical illness

There are essentially two types of life insurance: permanent and term. Depending on your goals and time frames, either type can be designed to cover these potential risks to your household.

Term is a relatively inexpensive option especially if you are young, healthy, and willing to commit to a specified time frame. You buy a policy for a fixed time period (say, ten to thirty years) with a fixed benefit amount (this is the amount the insurance company will pay your beneficiaries if you die). The younger and healthier you are, the cheaper the annual cost (i.e., the less likely the insurance company will have to pay the death benefit). With the policy comes peace of mind, knowing you are protected in the event of a premature death. But remember that term insurance provides coverage only for a stated period of time. If you do not die during that time period, then the policy expires and no benefits are ever paid out. A common downside of term insurance is underestimating the amount of time over which you'll need coverage. The upside: you are still alive and kicking!

Unlike term, permanent life insurance policies are designed with no specific time frame. They come in many varieties, but they all have similar objectives. Permanent plans are designed to last the lifetime of the insured and eventually pay out a benefit. They have a savings component commonly known as cash value. A policy's cash value can provide dollars for future goals. Permanent life insurance plans can also cover risks other than death. Many innovative insurance companies now offer accelerated benefits riders that can protect you in the event of disability or terminal or critical illnesses and even offer long-term care. These add-ons or riders can be included in the life insurance contract at a relatively low cost. Some term policies do offer similar coverage, but their limited time frame can be a drawback. Remember, term insurance is over a stipulated time period. What if you suffer a debilitating illness after your term policy has expired?

When purchasing life insurance, the older and less healthy you are, the more expensive the premiums. This could make the coverage cost prohibitive or put a crimp in your budget. Worse yet, you might be uninsurable. Yes, it does pay to stay in shape!

HOW MUCH COVERAGE DO WE NEED?

Answer: enough money to cover all your outstanding debts as well as enough to replace the income necessary to keep your plan moving forward. If you're on a tight budget and need a large amount of coverage, then term is probably the best way to go. However, if you can afford a solid plan that covers more risks, then permanent can provide additional benefits over time. I often recommend a combination of term and permanent for many of my clients. Here's why.

Earlier in life the term policy satisfies the risk of a premature death. This is the time when you're likely to have more debt (larger mortgage) and fewer assets. As you accumulate wealth and lower your debt, your risk then shifts to asset protection. You don't want a disability or a critical illness to wreak havoc on your game plan! A properly set up permanent plan can reduce this risk. Finally, a sound permanent insurance plan can help protect your wealth if you contract a chronic or terminal illness or require long-term medical care.

Deciding what type of life insurance and how much can be a tricky proposition. This is one of several areas where I recommend seeking out the advice of a trusted professional. (Keep reading—Chapter 18 is devoted to just that: how to find a quality advisor who can help you create your game plan for success. I've been in the planning industry for over twenty-five years, and there are both good and bad advisors. I will give you some tips and questions to ask during the interview process to increase your chances of finding a good one.)

7

WHERE DO WE WANT TO LIVE?

In my experience the average Joe and Josephine Smith care way too much about other people's perception. They're overly concerned about keeping up with those Joneses, whoever they are.

They want to live on the right side of the tracks, even if they can barely afford to cross over them. Or they want to be close to—or far away from—family, even if they can't swing it financially. So they bite off more than they can chew.

They don't admit it, though. Usually when I ask couples why they're buying a house that's well beyond their means they say, "We like the oversized bonus room. It will be great for parties!" Never mind that—oops!—they won't be able to throw any parties due to their overstretched house payment!

I understand the appeal of a big yard and a nice neighborhood, I do. But let's be realistic about what you can actually afford to spend. Now, I live in California, where real estate can be obscenely expensive for what you get. This applies to New York and other parts of the country too. So if $500,000 is your limit, living in one of the aforementioned states means adjusting your expectations and making decisions accordingly. You may even consider moving to a state where $500,000 gets you more bang for your buck.

Besides location, the home you can afford depends on the amount of money you make. My rule of thumb is: no more than 28 percent of your gross monthly income should go toward paying your mortgage, including property taxes and insurance. It's more conservative than what lenders will tell you, but when too much of your income goes toward the house payment, sacrifices need to be made in other areas. Are those sacrifices going to be yours? Hers? Ours? This uncertainty can lead to tension and animosity within your relationship.

An affordability-related issue that you need to be aware of is "price creeping," which can lure you in and prey on your emotions as it did to my friends Andy and Jessica. They owned a nice house for five years that suited their needs. Then one day they got "the price creeping bug": they wanted a brand-new house that was larger and in the most upscale part of town. They walked through the eye-catching model homes and decided to buy one of them right then and there, even though it was more than they planned on spending. In order to keep the new mortgage payment manageable, they had to roll all the equity from their existing house into the new one. But business was good, so they decided they could swing it.

They moved in and had a beautiful housewarming party; everyone, including the kids, was ecstatic. It wasn't long afterward, though, that Andy and Jessica's world was turned upside down. Andy's income fell just as the bottom fell out of the real estate market. Their mortgage payment became unaffordable, which put a huge strain on their marriage.

They had some tough decisions to make.

Sell the house? Easier said than done. Due to the market drop, all the equity—over $250,000—had vanished. They owed more money than they could get from selling the house.

Short sale or walk away? Both are extremely stressful and very damaging to your credit. Good luck trying to purchase another home in the future!

Renegotiate the loan? This is what Andy and Jessica chose to do. They contacted their lender and negotiated a plan that both parties could live with.

Andy and Jessica endured many a sleepless night agonizing over the unfortunate situation they got themselves into. It tested their marriage, but they are now determined to work through it together. They've told me time and again that they regret not staying in their original home with a mortgage payment they could easily afford that allowed for a lifestyle they surely miss.

Now that you've heard Andy and Jessica's tale of woe, here are some questions to ask yourselves to avoid becoming house rich and lifestyle poor.

Are the tradeoffs to owning a bigger, nicer home truly worth it? If something were to happen to one of you income-wise, would you be in a huge hole? Are you willing to shoulder the burden of stress that comes with living above your means?

Think back to the lifestyle you want to live. Some of those luxuries might need to be given up or realigned due to your new stretched mortgage payment. When you start to cut things out that bring you joy, this causes stress, which, in turn, causes arguments over whose luxuries to wave bye-bye to—yours or your spouse's?

Bear in mind that when you own a home there's lots of maintenance and upkeep as well. Who's going to mow the lawn? You, or will you hire a gardener or lawn service? If you have a pool, who's going to care for it? Do you like shoveling snow, or are you going to hire someone to take care of that for you? What about renovations, painting, and other projects? It all factors in, and it all costs money.

Here's another real estate oops I've run into, this one brought to you courtesy of my clients Rich and Amy. They were in their early thirties and wanted to live in a house with more land. That's hard to find in the coastal community where they were raised, at least not one that they could afford. So they moved inland, away from the water, where the lots tend to be larger, the houses bigger, and the costs cheaper. So far so good.

What they failed to take into account was the fact that Rich's job—he was a project manager for a tech company—was ninety minutes each way in heavy traffic at peak hours. That meant he had a three-hour commute round trip! Some people think they can survive that kind of commute, but nothing would make me more miserable than spending all that time in my car, driving to and from my office. I say this as a Californian, and you know how much we love our cars.

Lengthy commutes take a toll not only on your car—wear and tear, which costs money—but also on your relationship. If you're spending three hours a day driving to and from work, then eight hours a day at work, and perhaps an hour at the gym—when do you have time for each other? For your kids? Once again, what are your goals and priorities—is the commute worth it for the bigger house with more land?

Another question to ask yourselves is: How long do you anticipate living there? If you're a millennial, then you're most likely not thinking about settling anywhere anytime soon. Studies have shown that the younger generation expects to hop around to various parts of the country, partially because they like it but also because their careers might require it. They don't want be tied down to one specific town or neighborhood. If you plan on relocating frequently, then you need to factor that into your house-buying decision.

RENTING VERSUS OWNING

For some of you renting might be a smarter option. Until you have clarity on where you want to put down roots as a couple, renting makes some financial sense. Just like a mortgage, your rent payment should not exceed 28 percent of your gross monthly income. Renting is a "flat" expense in the budget—if the water heater breaks, for example, it's not your responsibility to fix it. Renting also gives you a chance to check out the neighborhood, the surrounding community, the area in general, and then determine whether you'd like to eventually purchase your home there.

When it does come time to buy, as I stated earlier, understand that your home is *not* an investment. Repeat after me: "My home is not an investment." It's your *home*. It's the place you live. If your home increases in value, your net worth has increased on paper, but that doesn't translate into cash in your bank account unless you sell it. And if you do sell it, *then* where are you going to live?

Real estate is what's known as a leveraged asset. Let's say you decide to purchase a $500,000 home. You put down 20 percent, or $100,000, and take out a $400,000 loan. If the real estate market increases by 10 percent, then your house is now worth $550,000. This means you now have roughly $150,000 in equity. But if the real estate market drops by 10 percent, then your house is worth $450,000 and you now only have $50,000 of equity. Remember Andy and Jessica, the couple who caught the price-creep bug? They put over $250,000 down on their new house, and the value subsequently dropped by more than that amount—that's a quarter of a million dollars in profits from the sale of their old house . . . gone.

HOW MUCH OF A DOWN PAYMENT DO WE MAKE?

Making a down payment of 20 percent or more can save you additional costs on your loan, as doing so eliminates the need for private mortgage insurance (PMI), which is usually charged to people who have less than 20 percent down on their home. Ideally you want more skin in the game and less debt on your balance sheet.

My rule is: the more you can put down, the better, assuming, of course, that the mortgage is in line with your budget. The target should be putting enough down to arrive at a payment that is 28 percent or less of your gross monthly income.

In time, with periodic raises, the original mortgage payment has a smaller impact on the overall budget. My parents are a great case study. They purchased their home in 1970 for $39,000. The monthly payment hovered around $250. As my dad built up his career year after year—bringing in more and more income—their mortgage payment became less significant, less of a burden. In turn, they had more money to spend on—yes!—those luxuries: his, hers, and theirs!

Just for kicks, ask your parents what their mortgage payment was when they bought their first house. Next, ask them what their monthly household income was that same year. (These answers will likely shock you!) I imagine their house payment took up a significant portion of their income at the time, but today that same amount is what you'd spend on a monthly car payment.

IS IT BETTER TO PAY CASH OR CARRY A MORTGAGE?

If you or your spouse has a wealthy parent, grandparent, aunt, uncle, or strange benefactor who wants to foot the bill, go for it. Just make certain you understand whether there are any strings attached. If you do have the financial wherewithal to pay cash for your home, just be sure you aren't getting yourselves into a situation where you are house rich and lifestyle poor. You still want to be able to adequately fund the rooms of your financial house— retirement, college savings, and so forth—and still have money left over for the luxuries in life, as this makes for a happier home.

If you're like most Americans, you'll have to take out a mortgage loan and assume a regular monthly payment. The mortgage interest on your loan is a tax deduction, which is a nice benefit. But taking out a bigger loan than you should, with the rationale that you'll have a higher tax deduction, does not justify buying a house you can't afford. As long as you *don't* bite off more than you can chew and you *do* live within your means, you'll be on the road to owning your house debt-free—whoopee!

8

WHAT IF ONE OF US LOSES OUR JOB?

Most of us think about disastrous events in the abstract, but we don't really expect them to affect us. Sure, intellectually we know that tragic, terrible things happen to other people, but *not* to us, so we don't properly prepare for them. For obvious reasons this is problematic, because you never know what the future has in store for you. Just pick up a newspaper or flip on the TV or hop on the Internet, and the evidence will smack you right upside the head.

You and your spouse must talk about and actually build that 911 Fund—the walls of your financial house. This fund needs to be a high priority in your game plan. Why? Because job losses happen and are real.

I experienced this firsthand early in my career. The company I worked for at the time decided to close my office without warning— suddenly I was out of a job. Bye-bye, income. Talk about a shock to the system! To make matters worse, I had just purchased my first condo and had yet to even furnish it. (Thank God for my uncle and his hand-me-down mattress set, and yes, it lay directly on the floor—no money in the budget for a proper bedframe!) I was single at the time and had nothing to lean on but my emergency fund. It wasn't long before I found a position with another firm, but not before going ninety days without a paycheck. Eliminating all my nonessential expenses and having my 911 Fund to tap helped get me through those anxiety-filled months.

I share that story with couples who don't believe it can happen to them. But it *can*, so you need to plan accordingly. Preparedness is the name of the game. (Have I stressed that enough already?)

So if one of you loses your job, besides looking for another one, what do you do? You'll need to sit down as a couple and review your budget. Go through it line by line and cross off all the items that are not critical expenses. Make sure you're on the same page as far as what those expenses are. Use the Highlighter Exercise to help you.

Then sit down and figure out how long you anticipate being unemployed. Ideally you'd find a new job fairly quickly. I always tell clients not to panic; instead, set out to find something better. (I did when it happened to me!) You'll want to call every contact you have as quickly as possible; after all, the longer you're out of the workforce, the harder it is to get back into it. Contacts diminish, and skills start to deteriorate.

Many times people lose their jobs and immediately look at their investment portfolio to make ends meet. But what if your portfolio is down in value at the time? Or, worse yet, you decide you want to cash in your 401(k) plan or pension fund—HUGE MISTAKE! There will be taxes and, if you are under age 59½, penalties on those dollars. Besides, you need that money for your retirement.

This is the time to tap into your 911 Fund; remember, it's the walls that keep your financial house standing. This fund was set up to use in the event of an unanticipated financial hardship, such as an illness, job loss, or natural disaster. Thanks to proper planning, your house remains in working order and is sound enough to weather the storm.

Warning! Your 911 Fund should *not* be used for some exotic vacation getaway or on some brand-new sports car you've been eyeing—the need to sun yourself and drive fast are not emergencies. I've met with countless couples who've wanted to use their 911 Fund for all the wrong reasons. I say to them, "If you were to spend it on a trip or a new car, how would you handle your finances if one or both of you were laid off next month?"

I don't mean to sound like a pessimist—ask anyone who knows me . . . I am far from it!—but at some point in your lives you will have an unexpected drop in household income. My job is to make sure you are prepared for that. I've seen the relief in my clients' eyes when they come in for a meeting after a job loss and I let them know we have a contingency plan in place. Planning and preparedness are surefire ways to keep the strain of unforeseen income loss at bay.

SHOULD I START A BUSINESS WHILE I'M UNEMPLOYED?

Now that you're not working you've got all the time in the world, right? So you might wonder whether it's a good time to do something radically different—like, say, open that gluten-free bakery you've been dreaming about.

It's an interesting dilemma. On the one hand, if you're forced into a situation you didn't want to be in—unemployed—then maybe it is God's way of giving you a kick in the pants. On the other hand, you can't just spend money willy-nilly during this time, especially if you and your spouse haven't evaluated the risks jointly.

The same applies to changing careers, by the way. In general, making a career switch usually involves pay cuts. There will also probably be a serious learning curve if you are entering a new profession. Are you willing to face those challenges? And how does your partner feel about it?

If you are going to start a business or switch careers, your spouse has to be on board with it. If they aren't, it's not going to work. You might have a successful business, but your family will be in tatters.

But okay, say your partner gives their blessing, and you write up a brilliant business plan. Before you do anything I'd recommend vetting it with a trusted advisor—or three. Not that I doubt your talents and abilities, but you definitely want to talk to someone who's got experience with starting a business. Even better, speak with someone in *that* industry. They'll most likely have interesting thoughts and ideas that never even crossed your mind before.

Is starting this business a passion or a financial opportunity? A major discussion point should focus on your new venture's ability to make money and support your game plan. Just because it's a passion of yours doesn't mean it's going to generate enough revenue to pay the bills.

My thirty-something clients Mike and Kori set out to follow their dreams of opening a high-end boutique, spurred into action after Kori was laid off from her job a few years back. Both had spent their careers working in the apparel industry—they were extremely knowledgeable in their field and eager to head out on their own. They did loads of research and created a detailed business plan. They talked to several trusted advisors before opening their doors.

The store got off to a great start, and sales were on schedule, with only a few unanticipated expenses. One challenge they faced was a "cash flow" crunch caused when several vendors required payment up front on merchandise yet to be sold. During that time they inquired about tapping into their retirement money, but after I explained the taxes and penalties, they decided against it.

Another stressful period arose when Kori became pregnant and was no longer able to work at the store full time. This meant hiring more help, which translated into more overhead. It was right around this time when Mike was offered a high-paying job, including health benefits, with a well-established fashion brand. After lengthy discussions together, they decided Mike needed to take the position because it would provide health coverage and much-needed cash for the household. This was extremely tough on Mike, as his heart was in running the business they had worked so hard to build.

Fortunately they've been able to keep the store, though they cannot be there to run it as they'd originally envisioned. Because of some good hiring decisions, the store runs smoothly and pays its bills, yet there's nothing left over to pay *them*. Mike and Kori took a huge risk in starting their own business, and at present they are getting no return on their investment.

Before taking the plunge with your hard-earned savings, it's important to evaluate the pros and cons. Mike and Kori are sensible and intelligent people who had a dream of owning their own boutique. It's great to have a dream of running your own business, but you need to evaluate its ability to succeed financially. You don't want to lose all your cash and even your credit without carefully scrutinizing all aspects of the endeavor.

Prior to starting a business it's important to ask yourself: Do we have enough "cushion" if the business starts out slowly or the economy takes a downturn? This is where having a healthy 911 Fund comes into play. Moreover, are we willing to put the time, effort, and energy into seeing it through? I have many successful business owners as clients, and all of them will tell you that it's not easy, but the rewards are sweet if you're willing to give it all you've got—and then some!

9

CAN WE AFFORD TO HAVE KIDS?

Far be it for me to tell people not to have kids because they can't afford them. But the truth is if you have not discussed each other's roles in raising your children, you could be setting yourself up for a different type of financial stress in your relationship. (Remember our lawyer couple Jed and Susie from earlier in the book?)

Many, if not most, people decide to have kids without a game plan in place. But let me tell you: you need a game plan. There are all sorts of things you have to talk about before having a kid.

Are we financially ready to be parents? When you decide to bring a baby into the world you have a responsibility as parents to love, nurture, protect, and provide for your child. Children, while being one of life's greatest blessings, also cost money, take up space, and consume lots of your time. Not having discussed how a life-altering event like parenthood will affect your finances, your home, your familial roles, and so on is just plain careless.

Take, for example, the couple who needs dual incomes in order to pay their bills. I see it all the time. Both people in the relationship are building their careers and making good money. They plan their budget accordingly, using both incomes to support a certain lifestyle. Their mortgage payment or rent is also based on two incomes. Then the baby arrives . . . congratulations! Soon afterward one parent decides to stay home or cut back at work. Bravo! However, along with that decision comes a drop in household income. Now what?

And what if, instead, you both decide to go back to work? Who's going to care for your baby—a nanny, day care, relatives? Unless you live near kindhearted family members who are willing to raise your baby free of charge, the alternatives cost money. Some people find that one spouse's income barely covers the cost of day care, which raises the question . . .

SHOULD I QUIT MY JOB TO RAISE THE KIDS?

Well, the first order of business would be to factor in all the expenses you'd be eliminating that would offset some of the income loss—child care, gas money, subway fare, dry cleaning, takeout meals, business clothing, and so forth. It may make more financial sense than you'd think.

I have pretty strong feelings about this, and I know some of you may disagree. As I mentioned earlier, I believe kids are one of life's greatest blessings. Next to marrying my wife, becoming a dad is at the top of my "best decisions ever made" list. I take great pleasure in it, and I take my role very seriously—spending time with them, teaching them, protecting them, providing for them.

Before starting our family Kendra and I talked at great length about how we wanted to raise our children and what kind of home life we wanted to provide for them. We both came from families where our moms stayed home, taking on part-time jobs here and there while we were in school. Our dads worked hard and did what they had to do to support the family. The stable, nurturing environment this created had a profound impact on our upbringing; we knew we wanted that for our kids as well.

For us the decision was easy: after the children were born Kendra would stay at home to care for them, and I would continue on with my career. Financially, we put ourselves in a position to make our goal a reality. We bought a house we could afford, fended off the price-creep bug, and made every effort to live within our means. Sure, having kids was an adjustment to both our lifestyle as well as our pocketbook, but we did not allow it to compromise the integrity of our financial house for lack of proper planning.

Now, Kendra takes her job very seriously too. She's in charge of the household, which includes being very involved in our kids' lives—their activities, their sports, their academics. Beyond the day-to-day benefits her role plays in our family, I think of her job as a stay-at-home mom as an investment in our financial future. Here's why. A study in the *Family Relations* journal found that children's academic success is associated with having mothers who frequently communicated with their children.[12] This entailed talking with them, listening to them, and answering their questions. When they enter their teenage years kids whose parents are home with them after school and in the evening are less likely to experience emotional distress.

The study goes on to say that kids whose fathers spend time doing activities with them tend to have better academic performance as well. Incidentally, I recently found myself having to brush up on my algebra and geometry skills in order to help my kids with their math homework. As Kendra often says, "It's like getting to relearn a different subject every day of the week!"

If your kids get good grades at school, if they test well and participate in an array of activities, their opportunities become more abundant.[13] This often leads to financial rewards—say, college scholarships—which, in turn, save you money. Ultimately, by capitalizing on those scholarships and attaining a viable college degree, this leads to better potential career opportunities. You get where I'm going with this? The investment you put in your kids when they are young benefits both them and you in the long run. It puts them on surer footing as they set out to make their way in the world, all the while being financially prudent for you and your spouse.

WHAT IF WE BOTH NEED TO WORK?

Two of my clients, Matt and Kim, came up with a smart solution to the stay-at-home dilemma. He's a golf pro, and she works in higher education. They recently had a baby, Carly, and they both need to work. In fact, Kim *wants* to work. She derives a large part of her identity from her career. And, under the circumstances, they needed her income to pay the bills.

There was no way they were going to be able to afford a full-time nanny. Day care was an option but not their preferred choice of child care. Lucky for them, Matt's parents offered to watch Carly two days a week. Additionally, Kim's mother, Bev, happened to be thinking about retiring from her job in the next few years, so Kim and Matt came up with a plan. Because Bev still needed an income yet wasn't married to her current job, why not hire her to watch the baby the other three days? Instead of paying a stranger to be a nanny, they're paying Grandma!

The grandparents are super-happy with their caregiver roles. Matt and Kim are happy because their daughter gets to be with family. And baby Carly? We can only assume she is thrilled being around all those doting people.

Knowing full well that they both wanted to work after the baby arrived, Matt and Kim made some lifestyle expense adjustments to offset the new child care cost in their budget. The transition went smoothly because, unlike our lawyer couple Jed and Susie, they had identified their postbaby roles beforehand—there were no surprises—and they worked out a plan that was both affordable and suitable for their family.

I understand that what works for one family may not be an option for another. But if you are *both* going to work, you *must* discuss your child care strategy ahead of time and start making the necessary financial adjustments to budget for the added expense. Sitting in the hospital together while cooing over your newborn is not the time to tackle this issue. It's a weighty one that deserves careful consideration well in advance of your baby's arrival.

WHAT ABOUT WORKING PART TIME?

This is a sensible option many couples turn to at this point in their lives. Certain employers offer a flexible schedule so you can work from home. Your job may not allow for that, but there are other employers who simply don't want to lose good employees, so they'll accommodate a part-time arrangement. Such was the case with our friends Karen and Art, who juggled the dual-income dilemma exceptionally well.

Prior to having kids each had a solid, well-paying career. Karen was working full time as a dental hygienist and Art was a lawyer. They knew they wanted a large family, and having Karen stay at home with the kids was a priority for them both. At the same time Karen felt strongly about continuing to contribute to their household income. So here's what they did.

After the first of their four kids was born Karen arranged to see patients only on Wednesdays and has been doing so for the past eighteen years. Nearby family members cared for the children on that day of the week, allowing Karen to continue her profession part time. For Art and Karen this was the plan all along, so they were already accustomed to living off of just Art's salary—there was never a big shock to the financial system. They had discussed their roles and family priorities in advance and planned accordingly, which, they'll tell you, was essential to finding a financial balance that worked for them.

There is no one-size-fits-all solution, but many times I meet with couples, and they've never really discussed all their options. They haven't evaluated how their decisions will affect the household financially—most notably, the affordability of their home. This gets back to my point that making a prudent home-buying decision is crucial. You must ask yourself: What if one of us wants to not work or slow down our career after we start a family—can we still pay our mortgage comfortably? This is where living below your means pays off. Can you see how communicating and planning early in your relationship can have a positive effect later on? Just as bad decisions have unfortunate consequences, good planning decisions can have a lifelong positive impact on your financial game plan.

IS IT WISE TO INVEST IN A CHILD'S TALENTS IN THE HOPES OF A SCHOLARSHIP OR FUTURE GREATNESS?

Probably not.

Let's face it: most of us who have kids believe we have a future PGA champion or Olympic gold medalist sleeping right down the hall. I know dozens of parents who are convinced—*convinced*—their son will be the next Jack Nicklaus or Derek Jeter, and they've spent thousands of dollars on lessons, camps, intensives, and so on.

Don't misunderstand me: I love sports, and I think it's great for kids to participate in them. I managed my son's baseball teams from kindergarten through junior high school, and I witnessed firsthand the positive impact sports can have on kids. They promote teamwork, discipline, and accountability. Sports teach kids greater life lessons, like how to deal with success and failure.

But here's the problem: as often as not, little Johnny isn't as talented as Dad thinks he is. Or, worse, the kid has zero interest in golf/soccer/volleyball/basketball, but Dad doesn't really care—Dad is focused on his own dream of having a sports star in the family, and he doesn't give a hoot how his son feels.

And so I ask: Wouldn't you be better off taking that $1,000 a month you're dedicating to sports and socking a portion of it into a college fund?

The same principle applies to music. Sure, it's wonderful to learn how to play instruments or learn how to sing. My mom's side of the family is all very musically inclined. But none of them became Taylor Swift or Justin Timberlake.

I advise parents to manage their expectations in regard to scholarships and/or moneymaking careers in these areas. It takes someone with extraordinary talents combined with uncompromising dedication to make it a possibility. If your child shows some talent and desire, then by all means explore additional training. But a word of caution: these trainers and training facilities can be very good, but they are also very expensive—hundreds, if not thousands of dollars a month—and they are a flourishing industry. It's in *their* best interest to tell you your child is awesome and needs to continue with intensive training.

So you need to ask yourselves: (1) Can we afford it? and (2) Does our kid realistically show the passion and skill? If the answer is no to either, cut your losses now. Your kid will be happier, you'll be happier, and your marriage will probably be happier as well. And, as we've established, I'm in the marriage-saving business too.

SHOULD WE SEND OUR KIDS TO PUBLIC OR PRIVATE SCHOOL?

Before you consider the private school option, once again, you must be able to afford it. This is where early planning matters. If you know you want to send your little bundles of joy to a private school at age four, then you better plan accordingly. Moreover, it would be wise to discuss as a couple the *type* of private school you each have in mind. What if one of you thinks Montessori school is the bomb, whereas the other despises the whole concept? What if one of you wants a Catholic education for your kids, but the other is adamantly against it? This is yet another topic that is best addressed early on in the relationship.

Next, *what is the value in sending our kids to a private school?* There has to be value in making those tuition payments. What is it?

Academics—Many private schools have rigorous academic standards that can better prepare your child to achieve higher SAT and ACT test scores, which lead to better university options.

Activities (e.g., sports, music, theater, student leadership)— If your kid is into band, some private schools offer exceptional music programs. Does your son love baseball? Find a private school that has a great reputation and is a good fit for his talent level.

Environment/community—This one is often overlooked but can have a big influence on your decision. Most private schools have some sort of religious component that reinforces good behavior and values. Parents choose—and are willing to pay—to have their son or daughter attend that institution. The families who opt to send their kids to these schools have a shared value system that often fosters lasting friendships.

I was blessed to be able to attend a private school for eleventh and twelfth grades. This gave me the opportunity to participate in activities that I would otherwise have missed out on had I remained at the much larger public school. Being in a smaller, more nurturing environment was a great experience for me. In fact, some of my closest friends today are ones I met in my last two years of high school.

But if private school is not an option or if you prefer to send your kids to a public school, then living in the right neighborhood with good school districts can pay off. Our kids had some wonderful teachers in the public school system where we live. We did our research not only on the schools but on the teachers as well. How do you find out who the good teachers are in your area? Ask around: talk to your trusted neighbors who have children older than yours. They will give you the scoop. If you can volunteer your time in the classroom (like Kendra did), you can see firsthand what the teachers are like and figure out which ones would be a good fit for your kids.

We all know there are good and bad teachers everywhere, even in private schools. The bottom line is that you need to be vigilant about staying involved in your kids' education. Go to the parent-teacher conferences! You'd be shocked at how many parents don't show up to these. Two of my sisters are teachers, and they have repeatedly told me that a big reason why kids suffer in the classroom is due to a lack of parental involvement. This always astounds me; after all, you brought these children into the world—it's your obligation to stay engaged and help them be the best they can possibly be.

10

WHAT'S THE BEST WAY TO TEACH OUR KIDS ABOUT MONEY?

This question perplexes parents more than the most uncomfortable "How do I talk to my kids about sex?" conversation.

For better or for worse, kids can learn about the birds and the bees from multiple sources—school, their friends, the Internet—but few places actually give them the real scoop on money management. (Not that they're necessarily getting the right information about sex either, but it's still talked about.) That's a shame, because if you don't learn proper money management skills when you're a kid, it's that much harder to learn them as an adult—and thus the need for a book like this!

You don't want your kids learning about money from their friends or strangers. It's *your* responsibility to teach them about money and, more importantly, how to make good decisions with it.

Kids learn about all aspects of life from their parents, and money is no different. You may not think they're aware of your behavior, but they are. They notice everything. They watch how you spend and save. They remember the "No, we can't afford that!" just like they hear you proclaim, "It's only money!" as you plunk down your Amex card. I often hear clients in their fifties, sixties, and older talk about how money was saved or wasted in their household growing up. It's stuck with them all these years, sometimes positively and sometimes negatively. In other words, the way we were raised influences how we behave in every arena.

When teaching kids about money it's important for both parents to be consistent in their messages. As we all know, if Mom says "no," then the savvy child is going to march straight up to Dad in the hopes of a resounding "yes!" And then what happens? Mom's ticked off at Dad, which isn't good for anyone.

Just like Kendra and I have Financial Date Nights together, we also hold periodic family financial meetings too. We started them when Tanner and Brooklyn were about twelve and ten years old, respectively. Maybe it sounds rather formal, but these meetings are really helpful. We use them mainly to educate our kids about money, particularly spending and saving. We've discussed how banks operate, what compound interest is, and, my favorite, the "Motske Matching Plan," where we "match" our kids on what they save, 25 cents for every dollar saved. Not only does it pad their bank account, but it also teaches them about interest and saving. Twenty-five cents on every dollar saved might seem too generous, but it provides a strong incentive to sock money away rather than spend frivolously.

Not surprisingly, we also discuss with them the perils and pitfalls of credit card use. This is critical. A report by Experian, the credit-reporting firm, found that millennials (nineteen- to thirty-three-year-olds) carry an average credit card balance of $2,682 and have the distinction of being America's highest card using generation—which I contend they earned because they simply haven't been properly educated.[14] They don't realize that credit cards aren't free money but rather thirty-day loans with exceedingly high interest rates!

Incidentally, Monopoly—yes, the classic board game with the car, the hat, and the boardwalk—provides an excellent teaching opportunity. It's fascinating to see what kids will do with their money. Some kids refuse to buy Park Place because then they won't have enough cash to pay their utilities. Or they worry about having to pay an expensive rent to a competitor on a space they may never land on. Others spend freely without considering the consequences. It's a great window into their psyches.

When we first started playing I asked my kids, "Why do you collect $200? What's that for?" They didn't know the answer. Neither do most people. It's actually your *salary*! (Clearly, it's an old game, created in 1934. Today that salary would enable you to live out of a cardboard box.) It's also a fun trivia question at a cocktail party. Monopoly has literally been played billions and billions of times, and still, nobody can ever remember what the heck it really means to pass Go!

But here's an interesting facet of the game: no one has ever won simply by zipping around the board and passing Go. The lesson is: you've got to take risks, invest, decide if you want to buy houses or hotels or not. And that's exactly like life. You're never going to get ahead if you just collect your salary, put it in the bank, and don't make investment decisions. It's a really valuable lesson for kids—and adults.

WHEN SHOULD WE OPEN THEIR FIRST BANK ACCOUNT?

Many couples take their kids down to the bank when they start receiving checks or cash gifts, such as graduation or birthday money. At the very latest it should be when kids get their first job, whether it's mowing the lawn, babysitting, or shoveling snow. This is a good time to teach them about interest, check writing, and how to use an ATM. Take them into the bank, cosign the forms with them, and walk them through the ins and outs of making a deposit. I believe the earlier you begin this process, the better. Kids who learn how to save and then begin to see their account balances rise feel a sense of accomplishment that encourages continued saving in the future.

When they do get their first job please take the time to explain how to read their first paycheck. Most of them will be amazed at how much taxes were taken out—I know a lot of adults are! My friend John has a sixteen-year-old son, Kyle, who got a job as a bus boy. He had worked six hours when he received his first paycheck. He was earning $8 an hour, so after a six-hour shift he expected to get $48.

What he hadn't learned about yet was this little tax called FICA, more commonly known as Social Security, or about state and federal taxes. Kyle was stunned that his total take-home pay was less than $40. But he looked on the bright side: "When I get my next check it'll be for a thirty-hour week, so I'll get $240!" he said. He forgot about the taxes again and quickly corrected himself, acknowledging he would have to pay another $8 in taxes, leaving him with $232. Kyle mistakenly thought a flat tax amount was taken out of every paycheck. He received a quick tutorial on percentages from Dad.

My friend had to explain to his son that taxes are a regular, weekly occurrence and that he could expect a sizable chunk to be extracted from his paycheck. Kyle was not happy about it—after all, who is? But now at least he understands the system.

SHOULD OUR KIDS MAKE A BUDGET?

Take a guess at what my thoughts are here. In a word: YES! I think everyone should make a budget, no matter how old. Or young. It's never too early to start.

When people—especially kids—earn their own money, they have a greater appreciation for it and are more discerning in how they spend it. So kids who have a job and have bills to pay can certainly benefit from making a budget. When it comes time to buy their first car, for example, they'll need to figure out how to budget for a monthly payment, insurance, registration, and gas, based on their income. So teaching them how to properly manage their money is important.

However, as tempting as it might be for you to manage it for them, resist! The idea is to let your kids make their own decisions, within reason. It's important for them to experience the consequences of their monetary choices. When it comes to discretionary purchases this usually goes one of two ways: they come to realize that what they purchased was a total waste of money *or*, because they used their own cash to buy the item, they value it more than if it were just given to them.

This is something I can speak to personally. My daughter, Brooklyn, loves Converse high tops and has three pairs, all in different colors. Not long ago she came across a new teal pair and just had to have them. I wanted to shout, "You don't need them! Your feet will grow!" Instead, I simply made it clear that if she really, really wanted them, she would have to buy them herself.

Now, it's one thing to want something knowing Mom and Dad are shelling out the cash for it; it's another thing entirely when kids must decide whether it's worth forking over their *own* money. More often than not they'll consider their decision more carefully and less impulsively. And if they do decide to go ahead and make the purchase, as Brooklyn did, they quickly learn about sales tax and the fact that the price listed on the bottom of the shoe is less than the amount they must eventually pay for the item.

As it turns out, Brooklyn wears her teal high tops quite regularly and took great pride in telling her grandparents that she bought them with her very own money! Difficult as it may be, resist the temptation to spit out the "you don't need that!" line; instead, turn these opportunities into teachable moments for your kids.

Having said that, I do believe you need to advise your kids how *not* to make choices that result in disastrous consequences. If you know they can't afford the car they are dreaming about, then you have an obligation to coach them out of making a terrible financial decision. If you can't sway them, you'll probably have the final say because you're likely cosigning for the loan. That gives you the opportunity to be the adult in the conversation and put your financial foot down. If you don't say no in these situations, then guess who'll be asked to bail them out when they can't make the payments or when a nasty repair bill comes due? YOU! Your kid paying $50 for a fourth pair of high tops that she really doesn't need is far different from paying $15,000 for a car she really can't afford.

SHOULD OUR KIDS GET AN ALLOWANCE?

The way I see it, an allowance is something your kids *earn* by performing chores around the house—cleaning up after the pets in the backyard, washing dishes, doing the laundry, taking the garbage out, vacuuming the house, and so on. It is *not*, however, an entitlement. They need to earn it.

In the course of helping a friend who hosts a weekly financial radio show I got the opportunity to interview Shannon Ryan. She's a certified financial planner who runs the Heavy Purse, LLC, a financial website for kids. She believes the word *allowance* is viewed as a form of entitlement. After listening to her explanation, I do think it's important to clarify what an allowance is and how it should be explained to your kids. Shannon offers a different alternative in her household.

Rather than paying out a fixed weekly allowance, Shannon created a "job board" for her household and posts regular jobs to be done around the house. The job board explains what each job entails and how much it will pay. Their kids have to qualify for the job and then complete it with a positive attitude in the desired time frame. (I love the attitude aspect.) At the end of the week Mom and Dad pay accordingly. Some may view this as a little extreme, but it does begin to teach kids about how money works in relation to a job and what they might expect from a future employer.

How much the kids should earn is another matter altogether. In my opinion an allowance should be proportional to the work being done. But the work has to be well executed, not half-hearted. They have to have a good attitude about it and not complain that they're too tired to lug the trash from the kitchen to the curb.

The amount also has to be proportional to what they are expected to buy with it. For example, if they pay for some of their clothes, then they'll need a greater allowance. You can always give them a "raise" as they get older and start incurring their own expenses.

Whether you pay a set allowance or create a job board like Shannon, the most important point is to begin teaching your kids the value of a dollar and the hard work it takes to earn one in society. I can assure you that getting them to understand the importance of saving, budgeting, and spending at a young age will pay dividends down the road.

11

WHAT'S THE BEST WAY TO GET OUR KIDS THROUGH COLLEGE?

Here is an unhappy fact: many four-year universities—room, board, tuition, books, and all that other good stuff—cost more than most people's first house. I paid $164,000 for my first condo. College costs today are approximately $20,000 a year for a public university and more than double that to attend a private one.[15] That's somewhere between $80,000 and $160,000 to put *one* kid through college! And that is for a senior graduating from high school today! Imagine what the costs will be five, ten, or twenty years from now!

Let's say you recently gave birth to a little boy or girl. The first thing on your mind is likely not how much college will cost when our bundle of joy turns eighteen. Yet the reality is that a newborn's parents can expect to pay upward of $150,000 to $300,000 for a college degree nearly two decades from now.

And what if it takes your kid five years instead of four to finish college? (This, by the way, is happening far too often!) Approximately

30 percent of incoming freshman graduate in four years from a public school and about 50 percent from a private one.[16] Well, do the math: that college degree just got 25 percent more expensive. Ouch! These numbers shock most people. They simply have no idea how pricy a college education really is.

I am a big advocate for finishing in four years. Do your homework. Some schools are so impacted—that is, heavily populated—that it's difficult for students to get the necessary classes to graduate in four years. Many schools will advise incoming freshman to take fewer classes so they don't get "overwhelmed and stressed out"! If your kids are getting stressed out in college with a full schedule, just wait until they get out into the real world!

I say to the parents, "Let's not pay five years of expensive tuition when it could be accomplished in four!" And although it's tempting to take out heavy loans to pay for your kids' education, DON'T DO IT! The last thing you want is for them to graduate with six figures of debt—or for you to take on that amount when you should be looking toward retirement. Unfortunately this is happening at an alarming rate. And I certainly don't want you to pluck any money out of your 401(k) plan. After all, there is no scholarship for retirement.

But don't despair!

A simple and effective way to start saving for higher education is through a 529 plan. These plans have nifty tax benefits and can be started for as little as $25 a month. This amount can be automatically drafted out of your checking account. It's quick, easy, and reliable.

But Jeff, you might wonder, is $50 a month going to put a dent in these steep tuition bills? I had a young couple, Rebecca and Tom, step into my office over twenty years ago. They had just given birth to their daughter, Tatum, and were interested in starting a college plan for her. We set up a 529 account into which they contributed

$50 a month, the amount they could afford at the time. Over the years they received raises at work and continually increased their monthly contribution.

Fast forward several years: Tatum graduated from high school with honors and was accepted to her college of choice. She received some academic scholarship money, but this still left Rebecca and Tom owing roughly $15,000 per year. Not to worry! We tapped into their college savings plan to pay the difference. Tatum went on to graduate from college with no debt and is building a great career in public communications. The moral of the story: when it comes to saving for college, just get started—the earlier the better still matters, and no matter how much!

If you already have school-age kids, I can't emphasize enough the need to start saving *now*! Doing so can prevent unwanted stress in your marriage later and ultimately help your kids get off to a fresh start after college, one that's free from all that student loan debt!

Another college financing option to explore is having grandparents gift money to their grandkids. Currently anyone (in this case, grandparents) can gift up to $14,000 a year to anyone (in this case, their grandchild). An excellent place for grandparents to gift money is into that 529 college plan I mentioned earlier. (We will go into more detail about gifting in Chapter 17.) My clients who have done this take great satisfaction in knowing they've made the college financial path a bit smoother for their grandchildren.

But what if my kids don't go to college? Many types of saving plans allow you to transfer an account from one sibling to another without penalty. In addition, most plans are fairly liberal on what they consider higher education expenses. The funds can be used for programs beyond the traditional college or university; tech or vocational schools fit the bill as well.

WHAT IF OUR KIDS ARE NEAR COLLEGE AGE AND WE CAN'T PAY?

Grants, partial scholarships, and loans exist to help in these situations. Have your child fill out the FAFSA form (Free Application for Federal Student Aid). You might qualify for some federal grants (free money) and/or subsidized loans.

A note about these programs: The majority of them are needs based. If you make a good living and failed to adequately plan for college education expenses, you are likely going to be very disappointed with the amount of "free money" you will receive. It'll probably be more loans than grants, but you and your college-bound student need to heavily scrutinize these loans. You could very well end up in a situation in which the state or federal government has unwelcome influence over your higher education decisions. As parents, *you* want to be in control of your finances and choices, *not* some bureaucrat. It's been my experience that people find themselves in these unfavorable financial circumstances not because they plan to fail but because they fail to plan!

Some Other Thoughts to Ponder and Discuss

Does your eighteen-year-old have a sense of what they want to do in life beyond school? Some kids have a clear vision of where they're headed—they want be a pilot or a teacher or maybe a veterinarian or computer programmer. But other kids have no idea. They head off to a particular college or university simply because that's where they got accepted. There is no carefully considered plan in place, which is not necessarily the worst thing early on. Plenty of kids start out with an undeclared major before they eventually find a field of study that really sparks their interest.

If you had asked me in high school what I wanted to be when I grew up, I would have said a professional baseball player. I earned a college baseball scholarship, the first step on my way to the big leagues! Needless to say, it didn't take me long to realize that the pro scouts weren't looking for five-foot-ten guys with average speed as their top draft prospects. I reassessed my interests, decided I wanted to pursue a career in business and finance, and then focused my studies accordingly.

In my case the area of study I chose to pursue had viable career options. What I caution you against is the kid who decides to get a degree in a field where the job opportunities are pretty much nonexistent or, worse yet, one in which they cannot support themselves. Why in your right mind would you pay tens of thousands of dollars for your kid to attend college only to have them graduate four (or five!) years later with no marketable skills?

The financial point I am making here is that if your student has no clue what they want to do, you and your spouse should evaluate your options.

DOES HAVING OUR CHILD ATTEND COMMUNITY COLLEGE FOR THE FIRST COUPLE OF YEARS MAKE MORE FINANCIAL SENSE?

This gives your kid an opportunity to hone in on a future career at a much more reasonable cost to you. After satisfying the general education requirements, your student can then transfer to the school of their choice, one that has a solid reputation for the degree they want to pursue. This approach will save you a whole lot of money. You incur expensive college costs for only two years rather than four. By the way, the degree handed out by a four-year university on graduation day is the same whether your kid went there for two years or four or more.

CAN WE AFFORD TO SEND THEM AWAY, AND ARE THEY READY TO LEAVE THE NEST?

Room and board is a significant expense to consider. I lived at home all four years of college, which was a reasonable option, as the school was a short fifteen-minute commute from my house. I'm not sure I would have done as well had I gone away to college right after high school; I believe I benefited from living at home—the full fridge and washer-dryer access were certainly a plus! My partial-tuition baseball scholarship helped, but it didn't cover room and board or annual tuition increases. Living at home was a huge money saver for my parents, especially because they had three more kids coming down the pike!

Yes, there's something to be said for the "college experience," which usually incudes living in a dorm or apartment with your pals. Many kids are mature enough to handle the transition and find that moving away heaps upon them experiences and responsibilities they would otherwise not have under their parents' roof. However, some kids leave the nest and spend their college years partying their socks off. This sort of college experience results in a lousy return on investment. You know your kid. It's your parental responsibility to assess what the best path is for them within your financial means.

BESIDES TUITION, WHAT FINANCIAL CONCERNS SHOULD WE HAVE IF OUR KID DOES END UP GOING AWAY FOR COLLEGE?

One area to address if you are sending your kids away to college is fiscal responsibility. Remember in the last chapter when we discussed teaching your kids about money? This is where establishing a budget and making sure they stick to it pays off. You don't want your kid repeatedly calling home, asking for additional cash. This can cause stress in your marriage, especially if you and your spouse are not on the same page! Mom might seem like the hero, sending Johnny an additional check here and there (unbeknownst to Dad), but in reality she is modeling poor financial behavior that will not serve her son well in years to come. Here's a little tip: enabling your kid—a legal adult one, I might add!—while undermining your spouse is never a good strategy.

Another financial pitfall to be aware of is the credit card solicitations that your college student is sure to receive. Credit card companies prey on college kids who are both desperate for money and gullible enough not to understand the risks. These kids are easy targets, especially if their parents have not taught them good financial habits. I've heard horror stories from exasperated parents whose kids have racked up debt they could not possibly pay back anytime in the near future. For a quick refresher on the dangers of excessive credit card debt please reread Chapter 3.

SHOULD WE CHARGE OUR ADULT KIDS RENT IF THEY ARE LIVING AT HOME WHILE ATTENDING COLLEGE?

My answer is no, but conditionally. Your kids' focus should be on their education. As parents, your focus should be on that too. So long as your kids are serious about their studies, are putting in their best effort, and are abiding by the rules in your home, consider college their job for the time being. Should they decide to shirk their academic responsibilities and spend their time frivolously, that's a sure sign they fancy themselves an independent adult and should then be treated as one. Start charging them rent immediately or send them packing. If your kid wants to behave like an adult, then they should have all the responsibilities of an adult, which *don't* include living rent-free in Mom and Dad's house. Remember, your job as a parent is to raise your kid into a self-sufficient, responsible human being, not a dependent leech, even if it requires tough love on your part.

SHOULD WE CHARGE OUR KIDS RENT IF THEY MOVE BACK HOME AFTER THEY GRADUATE?

These are the Boomerang Kids, and you've probably heard a lot about them recently. Heck, you might even be living near one! Our neighborhood is full of them. You know who they are: recent college graduates who went away to school only to return home four years later thanks to a lackluster economy or an obscure degree that makes it difficult to start a career. (Remember, the primary purpose of going to college is to be able to obtain gainful employment!)

This is often a tough situation for couples to deal with. You want to give your kids every opportunity to succeed, but you don't want to enable complacency.

My advice, first off, is to make certain that you and your spouse see eye to eye on this issue. You don't want the presence of an adult child in your home to adversely affect your marriage, financially or otherwise. That being said, don't feel guilty giving your kid as much love and support as possible, even financial, within reason.

If, however, you sense you're being taken advantage of, charge them rent and living expenses or give them a thirty-day eviction notice! There is no reason your twenty-two-year-old son or daughter should be living off of your largesse without contributing or seriously looking for a job. Quite frankly, it's not fair to you— or them. If they get too comfortable in their surroundings, they might very well lack any incentive to find work and head out on their own.

My client, Vivian, a mother of two, is currently grappling with this problem. Her older son, Jake, has been living at home with her since he finished college three years ago. She supports him financially—he doesn't contribute a dime—and he isn't gainfully employed. He drifts from menial job to menial job, doing whatever strikes his fancy.

Jake is milking Vivian like crazy, which, if allowed to continue, will negatively affect her retirement. She keeps enabling him by bailing him out, but it has to stop. At some point you've got to cut the cord.

If you do decide to charge your Boomerang Kid rent, as Vivian should be doing with Jake, how much to charge depends on you. That's relative to where you live geographically and what kind of resources you have. But one thing I know for certain: the easier you make it for them, the easier it is for them to stick around. At some point they must spread their wings, even if it results in a few hard landings along the way.

12

HOW DO WE DEAL WITH LIFE'S FINANCIAL PEAKS AND VALLEYS, ESPECIALLY WHEN THEY INVOLVE OUR KIDS?

I first met my clients Robert and Carol over twenty years ago. They were rolling right along the highway of life. Robert was working at a giant engineering conglomerate and putting money aside like a dutiful family man. They were loving, supportive parents to three kids who are all grown now. Reaching their late sixties, Robert and Carol decided they were ready to reap the rewards of years of hard work—they'd earned the right to relax.

Here's the problem: THEIR KIDS! Or two of them anyway— the middle daughter is married with children and is as responsible as they come. The oldest has incurred a series of health-related problems; he is constantly in and out of work, further adding to their financial woes—but it is Greg, the youngest, who has caused Robert and Carol the most angst.

A few years ago Greg moved out of the country, got married, and started a leather goods business; the young couple manufactured purses, belts, clothes, and so on. To start the company Greg got his parents—my clients Robert and Carol—to invest $50,000. They wanted to help their son reach his dream, so they made the investment and became partners—all with the best of intentions. But it wasn't long before one $50,000 investment became another $50,000 investment and another and so on and so on.

More than $250,000 additional dollars later the business has tanked, and Robert and Carol have depleted a sizable portion of their retirement account. They chose not to heed my warnings, blinded by the love for their son and the desire to help him succeed. Consequently Robert, now in his seventies, is working as a consultant just to make ends meet. And he is doing so at a time in his life when he should be enjoying his financial independence. Robert and Carol literally sacrificed their own happiness and financial well-being for their son.

I also have a client named Judith. She is widowed and has been enjoying a comfortable retirement while working part time in what I commonly refer to as a "fun job." A "fun job" is something you do in retirement that you enjoy, and it gives you a little extra spending money. Her only son, Mathew, called to say, "Mom, I am getting a divorce, and I need money to hire a good lawyer." Judith didn't want to turn her son down; she was fearful of not seeing her two grandkids due to the pending custody battle. It began as a $10,000 withdrawal out her retirement account. The divorce is now final—and Judith $45,000 poorer.

Oh, by the way, both Judith and Robert and Carol had to pay taxes on the $45,000 and $250,000 they took out of their retirement accounts. And neither son has the means to pay them back anytime in the near future.

Parents throw money their kids' way all the time when they are young, but after a certain age it's simply not smart. You can't sacrifice your own financial stability in a fruitless attempt to rescue your adult kids.

Here's a simple message for all you adult kids out there: don't ask your parents to bail you out! They have done enough already! It's hard for them to say no when these emotional situations are heaped upon them. Realize that if you take money from them now, you are jeopardizing their retirement. If they run out of money in their retirement years, you might very well be the one they come to for a place to live. I don't think you want that on your conscience, now do you?

THE STOCK MARKET IS DOWN AND . . .

"My daughter's getting married—I need to sell off some stocks to pay for the wedding." Hold on a minute here! You had to have some sense that this was an expense looming in the not-too-distant future. Now that the wedding fund is a fraction of what it once was, good luck telling your daughter that her dream wedding will need to be scaled down a little or, perhaps, *a lot*! As we discussed earlier, short-term dollars go in guaranteed short-term accounts, whereas long-term dollars are better suited for high-risk, long-term investments. The closer you are to using this money, the more conservative and liquid you need the money to be.

Note on weddings: I know it's a big day for the family and you want everything to be just right, but I caution you not to go overboard! Have a—do I dare say it?—*budget*. If the bride and groom simply can't stick to it, then (1) consider giving them a copy of this book as a wedding gift, and (2) expect them to supplement the additional costs. Heck, nowadays young people are waiting until much later in life to tie the knot, so they are much further along in their careers. Not only do they feel like they should at least chip in, some feel they should pay the lion's share. My point here is that paying for or participating in the cost of a wedding is a noble and kind gesture. Nonetheless, you don't want to find yourselves in "Wedding La La Land," a delusional place where all sound financial decisions are thrown by the wayside in pursuit of hosting the perfect wedding. Contribute what you have set aside for the blessed event and not a penny more—this is no time to sacrifice future retirement dollars.

WE ARE BEING SUED— WHAT SHOULD OUR FINANCIAL STRATEGY BE?

Yes, I've had clients who run a small business that have gotten hit with a lawsuit out of the blue; it's no fun and can be extremely stressful. Unlike a wedding, where you have a general sense that the expense is imminent, a lawsuit often hits unexpectedly, with the added uncertainty of not knowing whether you will eventually prevail in the case. I had to advise my clients to plan for an *anticipated* loss: act as if the loss were sure to happen. We reviewed their game and began reallocating dollars into liquid, guaranteed-type accounts. We were prepared for any outcome. In this case my clients won out and didn't owe anything (except some hefty legal bills).

But what if the stock market had dropped in the course of their legal battle (which took over three years) and they had lost their case? Now that's a double whammy! They'd have owed big money and would have had to sell assets in a down market to foot the bill. By setting aside money in an account not tied to the stock market, you reduce the risk of volatility. Once the legal battle is over you can always put those dollars back into the market.

WHAT ABOUT THE REAL ESTATE MARKET?
THE VALUE OF OUR RENTAL PROPERTY TANKED
AND WE LOST OUR RENTERS—NOW WHAT?

Don't put yourself in that position to begin with!

Remember when we discussed real estate being a leveraged asset? Just like the stock market, it can go up or down in value. Couples I meet with often inquire about real estate and, in particular, about rental properties. I know people who have owned rental property and reaped financial benefits. As you accumulate wealth it can be a way of diversifying your investment portfolio. But what happens when the real estate market drops? Simply put: surviving these inevitable downturns takes *time* and the intestinal fortitude to ride them out.

When purchasing rental property most couples take out a loan for a portion of the purchase price. This results in an additional payment in the budget. Ideally, you will then rent or lease the property for an amount that is greater than what you owe on it each month. Easy money! Sounds good to me, honey!

Let me tell you a story about Toby and Valerie, friends of mine who *love* real estate. Back in 2007 they owned a total of eight rental properties, which grew to be their main source of income. They were constantly refinancing the existing rental properties to buy more properties. After all, more rental income meant more spending money! Greed had completely usurped all common sense.

Living in California, where real estate is at a premium, I've seen this euphoria many times over the past twenty-five years. Couples like Toby and Valerie get caught in what I call the "leverage trap." They buy one property, and everything is working according to plan. Then they buy another and another and another! The value of the real estate continues to climb, and they are millionaires on paper! Life is good, and they are living the dream! What's more, as their leveraged real estate income rises, so does their spending. Want a new BMW? Why not?!

Again, it all looked good on paper for Toby and Valerie. The bank was willing to give them the loans, and they were able to afford the payments because their rental income was more than covering the difference.

Then the real estate market headed into one of its downturns, and the financial euphoria began to wane. They lost a couple of renters, and the game of "musical mortgages" started. When the music stopped they couldn't make the monthly payments on all their rental properties. They tried to sell them, but their leveraged equity was gone. (This is commonly referred to as being upside down.) Talk about raising the tension barometer in a marriage, especially if one of you was not aware of the risks associated with leveraged real estate.

Ultimately Toby and Valerie got divorced; the financial strain was just too much for the marriage to bear. In the end they couldn't reconcile their rental property obligations with the lifestyle changes they needed to make. Their credit was destroyed, and they both had to start over financially in their forties.

If you decide to pursue rental property as an investment and source of income, here are some questions to discuss as a couple:

- How long can we afford to make the payment without any renters?
- How much debt is "too much debt" for us to sleep at night (the Sleep Test)?
- Do we have money set aside for maintenance? (I love the couple who says they are going to be the "handyman" for their rental properties. This is usually short lived, as you normally have a day job that requires much of your time and attention. How can you fix things from your current job? What if the property is one hundred or more miles away?)

- Do we have additional money set aside for rental emergencies? (This should be above and beyond your 911 Fund!)
- Are we okay with being a landlord, or are we going to hire a management company that will cut into our profits?

Here's another way to look at real estate or rental properties: strive for low or no debt. If you have done your research on the location and pay cash for the rental property, then you have reduced your risk substantially. When you collect your rent, all the income, minus your upkeep expenses, goes into your bank account. If the real estate market drops, no big deal—we're still collecting rent! Renters leave—bummer! But we don't have a monthly debt payment, so we clean up the property and rent it again! If you want to invest in rental property, pay cash and enjoy the benefits of really owning the property. Just remember that excessive debt leads to sleepless nights and senseless arguments! Steer clear of it!

13

HOW DO WE TAKE CARE OF OUR KIDS AND PARENTS AT THE SAME TIME?

Welcome to the phase I'm entering and the reality for roughly half of adults in their forties and fifties.[17] We are known as the "sandwich" generation, and we've earned that moniker because we are sandwiched between kids who still need our help, and parents who may soon need our help. One in seven of us is *already* supporting our kids and parents financially, and I expect that number to rise. In addition to money, we divide our time between taking care of them and taking care of ourselves. Hectic? That's putting it mildly. And though you may not be "sandwiched" yet, you'll likely be there sooner than you think. Being proactive financially can ease the stress this life phase often puts on a marriage.

Let's discuss helping Mom and Dad first.

Many people don't have enough money to support themselves in their old age. Over a third of retirees live on their Social Security income alone, and only one in five adults feels they are saving enough for retirement.[18] Memo to everyone: start saving for retirement *now*! It's expensive.

Many older folks don't want to move after retirement—they want to remain as independent as possible. But for lots of retirees, just keeping up their residence turns into a physical challenge. Outside help then becomes a necessity or the house starts to fall apart. And what if you or a loved one does not live nearby? That means that at some point you'll need to hire caregivers to come by your parents' home every so often. If living at home becomes impossible for them and you do have to move Mom or Dad somewhere— say, an assisted living facility or nursing home—the facilities your state will subsidize are often bleak. Moreover, your parents must be completely broke to receive financial assistance; otherwise, they'll need to come up with the resources to pay for a nice living facility or else it'll fall on your shoulders. Either way, it's not cheap.

Oftentimes your parents have the financial resources to cover hired help or assisted living early on, but they end up outliving their money. Then what happens? Either downgrade their living facility or you start picking up the tab.

These can be gut-wrenching decisions because nobody wants to see their parents suffer. However, if it's going to damage your own financial house, then you need to look at all your options, including state assistance. Remember Evelyn, the woman who hid her poor financial decisions from her husband, Carl? Not only was Evelyn hiding the financial support she was giving to her parents (mistake number one), she was helping them way beyond her means (mistake number two). Evelyn wrecked her financial house and destroyed her marriage in the process. Learn from her mistakes.

Now let's talk about the kids.

Raising a family is not cheap; it requires your time and attention too. Many "sandwiched" parents have kids who haven't even entered or graduated from high school. This means you're still shuttling them here, there, and everywhere while also shopping for prom dresses and paying for driver education classes. In addition, your mother-in-law seems to constantly need help fixing the side gate, which actually needs replacing, but she doesn't really have the money to hire someone to do it, so it falls on you. And let's not forget that you've been considering flying your parents out to see their granddaughter star in the lead role in the school play because they wouldn't be able to afford it otherwise. Yikes! Where do we find the time—and money—to do it all?

Again, communication between you and your spouse is crucial at this frenzied stage in your lives. Never lose sight of the fact that you are a team, with a game plan, working together. It's as important to manage your time wisely as it is to prioritize your financial resources responsibly. Divvy up the duties so one of you is not bearing an inordinate amount of the burden, to the detriment of the family unit. Keep in mind too that your kids are watching and, if not watching—because that would require lifting their eyes away from their phone screens!—are being affected by how you handle this generational juggling act. When they see you driving Grandpa to and from his doctor appointments or buying extra groceries to stock Grandma's fridge yet all the while you're right there by their side at night helping with the homework or taking them to the sporting goods store to buy a new pair of soccer cleats, they'll remember. So when *their* "sandwich" time comes you can rest easy knowing you modeled good, responsible behaviors, both emotionally and financially, and feel confident that they will pay that forward to you.

Some of you are "sandwiched" between helping Mom and Dad and your adult children. Studies show that a majority of people feel a greater responsibility to help their elderly parents rather than Johnny, who is twenty-eight and can't figure it out financially.[19] Believe me: I have many clients who have a hard time saying no to Johnny, but more often than not Johnny needs to be left to his *own* devices and make his *own* way in the world. No matter the age of your kids—eight, eighteen, or twenty-eight—you only have so many dollars to go around for their needs, your needs, and your parents' needs. So you *must* sit down with your spouse and determine how you want to allocate those dollars. You're not the US government, so you can't print money, and going into credit card debt isn't the answer either. Work within your means to reach a solution you both agree on. You'll be happier for it.

Here's my story.

My kids are approaching college age—we have already discussed the financial hurdles there—and my parents and in-laws are all in or around their seventies. I want them to live well into their nineties and beyond, but at some point I know I'll need to help them with various transitions in life.

When discussing this topic I like to use the word *transitions*. Why? I have used this term with clients over the years, and it strikes the proper tone with them. We're usually dealing with gradual shifts in life versus major adjustments.

Let's begin with *transition one*, when you notice your parents are slowing down a bit or you see that they *should* be slowing down. They might even still be working, but at the end of the day they seem a little more tired than they used to be. This is the time when they could use more hands-on help—assisting with tasks around the house, fixing things, or checking in on them more frequently than you had in the past. You can pay a handyman or a cleaning lady to help or you can do it yourself.

My parents, who have been "empty nesters" for years, still live in the five-bedroom house where I grew up. Kendra and I pay to have their house cleaned twice a month. Why? I noticed how exhausted my mom seemed to be trying to balance work, caring for her grandchildren, pursuing her own outside interests and keeping the house ship-shape. My parents would never hire someone them-selves, so we presented it to my mom as a Mother's Day gift. This was a nice and somewhat subtle way to get her to agree to it. She's a hard worker and has always taken great pride in maintaining her home, which I admire about her, but it was time.

Now, I'm not a "fix it" type of guy, but Kendra can fix anything. She puts this talent to good use at my in-laws' house on a regular basis. Another bonus: our kids are great helpers when they're at Grandma's—gardening, cleaning the pool, washing the windows, picking the berries . . . you name it. If only we could get them to help out that much at home!

What if our parents live far away? If you don't live within a rea-sonable driving distance from them, your help will likely have to come in one of two forms: (1) making arrangements with local friends or church members in their community to look in on them and offer assistance as needed, or (2) hiring professionals to take care of their additional needs out of the money you've set aside for this very purpose, knowing full well that when the time came you wouldn't be able to just "pop in" and help. And do I even need to reiterate how this can be achieved? By building a sound financial house, of course!

It's important to keep in mind that as you become more ac-tively involved in your parents' lives this transition can set off a whole host of emotions for them: gratitude, guilt, perceived loss of control, and so on. Be sensitive to it. In most cases it stems from a deep-seated desire to remain independent, to not become a burden on the family. Though they may resist the gestures of help early on, I believe if you are doing it in a loving and caring way, they'll come to see that you have their best interests at heart. Oftentimes gradual involvement is far more effective and more readily accepted.

Just be careful not to ruin your *own* finances in the process, a fate that befell my clients Daniel and Kate. Their financial woes resulted from a mix of deception and cultural differences. Daniel is Filipino, whereas Kate is not. In Filipino culture it is the children's responsibility, particularly the oldest son's, to care for his aging parents. (By the way, this is not a tradition exclusive to that culture.) As it turns out, Daniel's parents, who still lived in the Philippines, were flat broke. Daniel took it upon himself to begin sending them money despite the fact he had never discussed the issue with Kate. Problem number one: a lack of financial transparency!

Daniel reasoned that it was a modest amount, one that his wife didn't really need to know about because it would have little impact on the family budget. But after a while, as aging parents often do, his mom and dad began incurring medical charges that required attention. What now? Daniel didn't have the additional funds lying around to pay for these expenses. So he did what many people do when they can't afford something: he opened up a credit card in his name only (see problem number one) to cover the costs.

Problem number two: you simply shouldn't spend what you truly can't afford. By opening up a new credit card to pay for his parents' medical bills, Daniel was merely playing a shell game, one he surely would not win.

Problem number three: pride got in the way. Daniel's parents were unaware that he was digging himself and, therefore, his family into a deep financial hole. Out of a strong desire to help, Daniel gave his mom and dad the impression that he was far more capable of assisting them than he actually was—a triple whammy of poor decisions that resulted in a huge strain on both his finances and his marriage.

Before even thinking about helping others, whether it's your parents or your kids, you need to be in a stable enough financial position to do so. If you're struggling to *pay yourself first*, then you have no business paying for somebody else. As the flight attendants always remind us prior to takeoff: in the event of an emergency place the oxygen mask on yourself first before attempting to help others. Great advice, and the same goes for your finances.

SHOULD OUR PARENTS CONSIDER DOWNSIZING, OR "RIGHTSIZING," THEIR HOME?

I get this question frequently during planning sessions. Although it may make a lot of sense for them financially, many people have a strong emotional tie to their home, especially if it's where they raised their kids, that prevents them from embracing the idea. When approaching this topic with your parents, I always recommend a subtle approach, highlighting all the potential positives of making a move. Here are a few, in no particular order of importance:

- Moving to a single-story dwelling will make it easier for them to get around.
- Getting involved in an "active" senior community will expand their social life.
- Being closer to family will make it easier to see the grandkids.
- Unlocking any built-up equity in the home will give them money.
- Improved weather conditions are a possibility—unless they move to Alaska!

By the way, I often use "rightsizing" verses downsizing in meetings. It softens the topic a bit and sometimes even brings about a chuckle or two from those involved in the discussion—financial humor.

Next comes *transition two*. This is when you or your parents recognize that they could use more help than the family can aptly provide. Their day-to-day needs aren't being met or perhaps one of them has already passed away, leaving the other in need of outside care. During this phase your parents are often still living at home, which is where they'd usually prefer to be. If you haven't discussed the rightsizing option yet, now would be a good time to do so. They may require some part-time medical assistance at this point, but it only takes one life-changing event—a stroke, a heart attack, a broken hip, a cancer diagnosis—for that to turn into full-time care.

"Well, Mom or Dad could just move in with us . . . "

It is the rare occasion that this pours from the mouths of both spouses simultaneously; it's usually put forward by one and knee-jerkingly rejected by the other. This is a sensitive subject and a tough one in terms of compatible responses. When one spouse says in our meeting, "Mom will just move in," and the other says, "Yeah, that's not going to happen," the shock, anger, hurt, and defensiveness is written all over their faces. Not once had they broached this topic before, even knowing full well that Mom was already suffering from early signs of dementia.

This can be a contentious issue among siblings as well, trying to figure out whose home Mom or Dad will end up in. Yours? Your sister's? Your brother's? Shared time among the three? Communicating often and openly as one big family unit will help you determine the most viable solution.

This brings us to *transition three*, the most challenging and difficult for most families. During this phase Mom and Dad can't take care of themselves and require full-time in-home care or need to move into an assisted living facility. Let's go down the list of alternatives in decreasing order of desirability:

Remain in their home with professional caregivers present around the clock: It can be quite costly, but one advantage is that Mom and Dad get to stay in comfortable surroundings.

Move into an assisted living facility: These are *not* nursing homes. They are residences for the elderly and can have the look and feel of a nice home or apartment. Although they don't provide medical care, they can offer assistance with daily activities.

Move into a nursing home: This is the alternative that elderly people fear most. These facilities tend to have the look and feel of an institution or hospital. They are designed for people who need detailed medical attention and cannot care for themselves.

As you wrestle with the various professional-care options, do your homework and talk to people, especially those who have been in a similar position. Make sure the services provided fit your parents' wants and needs, not just what *you* think is best for them. And, as always, you need to factor the costs into your decision, even when it's one you'd rather make straight from the heart.

I've sat through many of these planning meetings in all of the various stages above. I have met with the elderly parents to discuss their future plans and with the kids to discuss their parents. I have also had a joint meeting with everyone in the same room. It's hard to predict life's turns, but either which way, the families who have a game plan prior to necessitating a decision are far better off than those who don't.

My clients Ralph and Marilyn are a lovely ninety-something couple who spent their eighties happy, healthy, and independent. Along the way I had been meeting with them as well as their daughter and son-in-law to help them plan for the next phase of their lives. About a year ago it became evident that Ralph and Marilyn could no longer care for one another on their own, so they moved into an assisted living residence. Ralph fought it tooth and nail; he went in kicking and screaming because, in his mind, he and Marilyn had been managing well enough.

But Ralph eventually came to terms with the inevitable. The planning and open dialogue beforehand paved the way for a smooth transition. Today he and Marilyn are thriving in the place they now call home. They've made some friends, and in hindsight Ralph sees the wisdom in their move, one that has brought peace of mind to the whole family.

The demands—emotional, financial, and otherwise—of helping both your kids and your parents can be unsettling without careful planning and thoughtful communication between you and your spouse. It's imperative that you make time for your Financial Date Nights—they can be the calm amid the chaos. Some couples even grow stronger in their relationship, gratified by all the good they're doing for the people they love most.

14

JACKPOT! WHAT DO WE DO IF WE INHERIT A LARGE SUM OF MONEY OR GET A SUDDEN WINDFALL?

This sounds like a no-brainer: What could be bad about coming into unexpected cash, like an inheritance? Yippee!

Many people have a similar reaction when a sudden windfall comes their way: spend, spend, spend! They think that acquiring things—expensive cars, fancy clothes, new houses—will make them happy. It won't. It's merely a temporary high often followed by a devastating low once the money runs out.

The *sensible* reaction would be to take a deep breath and review your financial situation. Spend wisely. Be prudent. It should come as no surprise that I don't want you to spend it all at once; instead, I want you to objectively examine what you hope to accomplish with this particular chunk of change. Analyze your debt and figure out where this money can best help you in the future. If you've got a slew of bad debt, pay that down or off entirely. If you're behind on college funding, sock it there. If you don't have any money set aside for retirement, put it in that bucket. In other words, put this money toward those parts of your overall plan that are the weakest. It's important that you take the time to look at the bigger picture and prioritize your needs and goals.

It's been my experience that people who sensibly manage an inheritance deeply respect the person who bequeathed the money to them. They approach it with a certain gratitude and reverence, whereas those who simply feel entitled to the money are a little more cavalier in the way they handle it.

Elsie, a longtime client of mine, was ninety-five when she died. She was a Depression-era baby and deathly afraid of losing her money. Any investments we made had to be extremely safe. She was a big fan of certificates of deposits, also known as CDs.

After she passed away, her sons, Ted and Martin, who were in their sixties by that time, each got half of her estate. Ted, who was single, had moved in with his mother and spent a lot of time caring for her. Martin, a married man, was very involved in Elsie's life but was still helping his kids too. Sound familiar?

When it came down to managing the inherited money, Ted went with a cautious, careful, risk-averse approach. Although that strategy made perfect sense for his mother, it made little sense for him. He was still a relatively young man with financial goals and dreams, so putting the entire amount in a savings account bearing little interest was not the best way to reach them. He had spent a tremendous amount of time listening to his mother and, thus, had adopted her investment philosophy as his own. But Elsie was in her nineties and Ted in his sixties—different circumstances require different investment strategies.

Ted's younger brother, Martin, who's retired with a wife and kids, has been a client of mine for over twenty years. When it comes to their family game plan, he and his wife, Jan, have always followed my advice to a T, which is why I was a little surprised when he seemed reluctant to allocate his inheritance as I had advised. Much like Ted, Martin was hesitant to do anything risky with the money; he was emotionally attached to it. Martin felt like it still belonged to his mom and he didn't want to blow it.

In the span of a year I was able to get both Martin and Ted to think through where their money *should* go, where it would logically serve them best. I felt confident telling them so because I knew that's what Elsie would have wanted. Over time it became less "Mom's money" and more their own.

Professionally the recommendations I made for their money were fundamentally sound and should have been implemented immediately. But personally Ted and Martin weren't ready to follow through on it, so we had to take it slowly, one step at a time. I had the privilege of working with their mother for over twenty years. Elsie did a lot of things right in raising her two sons. They respected her and, therefore, were determined to treat the money she handed down to them with equal regard.

Then there's my former client, Doris, a retired school administrator, a good saver, and all-around great lady with four kids, all of whom are financial train wrecks. She too died in her nineties, and her family could barely wait for the coffin to be lowered into the ground before contacting me. They were chomping at the bit to get to "their" money. Compared to major estate inheritances, it wasn't a huge amount, about $400,000 total, but each one of them blew through their portion within six months. They paid off their credit cards, which I suggested, but it wasn't long before they were ratcheting them up again. It was upsetting for me to watch them fritter their money away.

Frank and Eileen's story is one with another woeful ending. The first time they came to see me this couple was in major financial disarray. His business had gone south, and although Eileen was working, her income was not enough to support their expenses. They had tons of credit card debt and hadn't paid the IRS in years.

Then Frank inherited $1.9 million.

Early on they took my advice: this was an opportunity to get back on track. They paid down a lot of their debt, started to repair their credit, got caught up on their back taxes, and set up college funds for the kids. All was well in the household.

They still had a large sum of money left. I wanted them to invest it, but they wanted to buy a house instead. I suggested they lease for a while until their credit rating improved or else they would have to pay cash for the house—bye-bye 911 Fund! But Eileen fell in love with a charming fixer-upper, which was beyond their price range to boot. They bought it anyway, paid cash, and spent thousands more renovating it. Then the storm hit: Eileen was laid off from her job right about the time Frank's business went belly up. It wasn't long before they drained the rest of their account in full.

During this time I reached out to Frank and Eileen regularly to go over their finances and address the concerns I had with their overall plan. Not long ago I had received an e-mail from them saying, "We have to sell the house." I was not surprised. They'll get some money back, but they ruined an opportunity to get their financial house back in order.

I share these stories not because I want to scare you (well, only slightly!); I merely want you to avoid ending up in similarly dire circumstances.

WHOSE INHERITANCE IS IT?

Speaking of sharing, you don't *have* to share your inheritance with your spouse if you don't want to. Now, I'm not advocating this—it doesn't really build trust—but legally you are not obligated to do so. The bequeathed money can go into your very own bank account, and then it's yours alone. The minute you do decide to share it with your spouse, though, it becomes both of yours. So if you ever split up, the money would get divided equally between you.

WHAT ARE THE TAX IMPLICATIONS?

In most inheritances the estate (or living trust) pays the death taxes before you get your pay out, so an inheritance is commonly a "net" number to you. There are exceptions, including some inheritances that can increase your income taxes (like receiving an IRA distribution). You'll want to have a tax or legal professional look at what you've received to ensure that you don't need to withhold any money. Ditto for gifts—generally the giver pays any gift tax that's due.

But lottery and casino winnings are a whole different story. Unlike most inheritances, you will be responsible for ordinary income taxes on the money you win and possibly other taxes as well. These rules vary greatly from state to state, so if your winnings exceed $5,000, you must consult a professional before making a major move with this money.

A Final Note on Inheritances

Don't count on getting one. Too many of us expect to receive a great big financial windfall someday, but that's a pipe dream for most and foolish planning at the very least. People are living much longer these days and are electing to spend their retirement nest eggs on themselves.

I have a client with an eight-figure net worth—that's a whole lotta zeros! For his own reasons he has decided to leave only a modest amount of that to his kids, and the rest he's donating to various charities. It's *his* hard-earned money, the upshot of building a wildly successful business. Now, he loves his kids, but he feels they should create their own path to financial success, as he did. I encouraged him, however, to discuss his plans with his children in order to prevent any unpleasant surprises once he's gone.

The moral of the story? Don't expect a dime. But if dimes *do* come your way, identify the weaknesses in your financial house and use that money to shore it up before you even think of spending it all on fancy upgrades.

15

WHAT DO WE NEED TO CONSIDER BEFORE WE RETIRE?

The number-one question people ask themselves when contemplating the idea of retirement: Do we have a large enough nest egg to retire comfortably? More often than not the fear of running out of money is lingering somewhere in the back of their minds. They are really excited to retire—they've been working toward it their whole lives—they just don't want to have to *un*-retire.

It's wise to be concerned, as most of us haven't saved up enough to leave the work force indefinitely. According to a recent survey by Americans for Secure Retirement, 88 percent of all Americans are worried about "maintaining a comfortable standard of living in retirement"—up from 73 percent in 2010.[20]

Now is the time to *look*—for help from a financial professional—before you *leap*—into retirement. Sure, there are places online where you can plug in how much money you have, and they will crunch the numbers and spit out a formula for you. The problem is that those sites are often set up by companies trying to sell you a particular product. Furthermore, their projections might be rosier than a professional's would, which can leave you with a false sense of security. This is your *retirement* we're talking about, and you need serious retirement advice. There's simply too much riding on it—your serenity, your security, your sanity! The last thing in the world you want to do is quit your job only to have to hunt for another one years after you'd thought you left the workplace for good.

I cannot emphasize this enough: retiring is not some pie in the sky decision. It's a serious undertaking. I use a calculation called the retirement income estimator (RIE), which takes into consideration your current monthly income today and adjusts it for inflation in order to determine your future monthly income needs. For example, if you make $6,000 a month in today's dollars, how much will you need to earn thirty years from now, assuming a 3.5 percent inflation rate, to buy the exact same amount of "stuff"? How does approximately $17,000 sound? Pretty alarming, I'll bet.

You *will not* be able to maintain your same standard of living thirty years into the future earning the same income you do today. Inflation takes a big bite out of your purchasing power by causing the cost of goods and services to go up. At 3.5 percent that iPhone you bought for $200 last week will cost you $561 when you retire in thirty years. Your $2,500 house payment becomes a $7,000 obligation. The $6,000 a month you're currently bringing in wouldn't even cover the cost of your mortgage come retirement. The point here is this: in order to keep the lifestyle you currently enjoy today once you retire, you'll need to save more than you might think.

Note to younger couples: *Time* is an advantage you never get back once it's gone. The earlier you and your spouse start planning for retirement, the further along you'll be in staying ahead of inflation and in making your way down the road to financial independence.

DO WE HAVE ENOUGH MONEY SAVED
TO RETIRE AT SIXTY-FIVE?

In order to come close to maintaining the lifestyle you have today, you must be able to generate at least 80 percent or more of your current income. So if you're earning $8,000 a month now, you need to make a monthly sum of $6,400 in retirement to maintain your present lifestyle. This is important to plan for because both you and your spouse will be frustrated if your standard of living decreases significantly. Rather than making the most of your retirement years, you'll spend them scurrying around trying to figure out how to make up that lost income. That's no fun. And you certainly didn't work for thirty or forty years to take a lifestyle pay cut.

Retirement can be deceptively more expensive than people realize for the simple reason that you suddenly have an additional forty hours (or more!) per week to *spend money*. Those hours and hours of free time often morph into hours and hours of spending freely. So before that happens, MAKE. A. BUDGET. That's right! You need to know what your projected income and expenses will be *before* you decide to retire. (By this point you should know that you need to think about life as one giant budget.) The same rules apply as always: separate the wants from the needs, the negotiables from the absolute must-haves. (Again, you can refer to the budget worksheet in the back of the book as your guide.)

Within that budget the cost of health insurance must be taken into account. At age sixty-five you become eligible for Medicare. Medicare has two basic parts: Part A, which is hospital insurance, and Part B, which is medical insurance. The cost is roughly $100 per month *per person* for both Part A and B combined. Then there are add-ons to your basic Medicare coverage, also known as "Medigap" plans, that you can pay for separately. These cover additional expenses such as prescription drugs or deductible costs.

One important note: Medicare does not cover long-term care costs. You need to purchase a separate long-term care policy or a life insurance policy that has a long-term care rider to help protect against this risk during retirement. All your medical costs need to be factored into your overall retirement budget.

Another issue to consider regarding health insurance and retirement timing is the age of your spouse. If your spouse is under sixty-five (not qualifying for Medicare) and currently covered under your employer's health plan, then it might be in your best interest to delay retiring until Medicare coverage kicks in for your partner.

Once you've taken a look at your health insurance costs, next you need to determine your guaranteed monthly income at retirement. For some people it starts with examining their pension plans.

Pensions are a dying breed, so if you have one, you are the exception to the rule. Today the bulk of them come from either government or union jobs. Pensions provide a guaranteed income to you and your spouse as soon as you hit retirement age, and it lasts for life. Nice perk if you can get it.

But most Americans can't. Most Americans need to create their own. You could argue that Social Security is like a pension, but that's hardly a consolation. In case you haven't heard, Social Security is running out of money. As the American population continues to age, more money will be going *out* of the system and less will be coming *in*. I counsel my clients *not* to rely on Social Security as their primary means of retirement income. I've met retired couples for whom this is in fact the case, and believe me, it's not a lifestyle to which you should aspire. Social Security should be a supplemental pension at most; think of it as a bonus from the government.

WHAT'S THE OPTIMAL APPROACH TO TAKING OUR SOCIAL SECURITY, AND WHEN SHOULD WE BE DOING SO—EARLY IN LIFE OR LATER?

There are several factors to consider, most pointedly your health and your income. Are you healthy? Still working? Is your spouse employed? How does your balance sheet look? Do you need the Social Security income to survive, or can you defer it to receive a bigger check in the future?

Social Security is a really complicated system; it confuses a lot of people. You need to be very careful when and how you take it. In golf parlance: Social Security doesn't give you a lot of mulligans. For you nongolfers, that means you don't get many do-overs. Once you've begun taking distributions you get a one-time change, and it has to be made within the first twelve months. After that you are locked into whatever plan you picked.

You can begin taking Social Security at age sixty-two, and although many Americans choose this option, it's rarely a financially sound one. I understand the reasoning—they've been paying into the system forever, and they want to start getting paid back. This rationale works if you are unhealthy, you *really* need the money, or you think you'll die early into your retirement. If any of these apply, then by all means, take the money and run. However, if you are in relatively good physical shape or have longevity in your DNA, you're likely to get *more* money out of the system by deferring your benefits as long as you possibly can, because Social Security pays you interest for waiting to opt in.

Clarifying exactly how Social Security distributions are calculated would involve subjecting you to a long-winded explanation of seemingly ever-changing formulas brought to you courtesy of the federal government. And although that sounds like a blast and a half, covering some of the basics should be enough to leave you feeling smarter than the average bear.

Social Security benefits are computed using a figure known as normal retirement age (NRA), a number between sixty-five and sixty-seven, depending on your birth year. Find your NRA in the chart below.[21]

The NRA, along with wages earned and years worked, are factored together to arrive at a baseline benefit amount. This is the amount your Social Security check would be each month over your lifetime if you started taking distributions at your normal retirement age. You can go to the Social Security website (www.ssa.gov) and plug in your information to get an estimate of your future benefits.

To see how this works, take the following example. Imagine you're sixty-two years old. After looking at the chart you discover

NORMAL RETIREMENT AGE

Year of birth	Age
1937 and prior	65
1938	65 and 2 months
1939	65 and 4 months
1940	65 and 6 months
1941	65 and 8 months
1942	65 and 10 months
1943–1954	66
1955	66 and 2 months
1956	66 and 4 months
1957	66 and 6 months
1958	66 and 8 months
1959	66 and 10 months
1960 and later	67

Notes:

1. Persons born on January 1 of any year should refer to the normal retirement age for the previous year.

2. For the purpose of determining benefit reductions for early retirement, widows and widowers whose entitlement is based on having attained age 60 should add 2 years to the year of birth shown in the table.

that your NRA is sixty-six. Let's assume your baseline benefit amount came to $2,000. That means that if you waited four years, until age sixty-six, to begin receiving Social Security at the normal retirement age, your monthly check would be $2,000 for life.

But what if you decide that you need the money *now* so you start taking distributions four years before your NRA, at age sixty-two? Then your lifetime Social Security check would drop to a fixed $1,500 each month, a 25 percent reduction from the baseline amount. On the flipside, suppose you plan on working awhile longer and opt to put off taking your benefits until age seventy. For each year past your NRA that you defer getting a Social Security check, up to a maximum age of seventy, you receive an 8 percent compounded credit (less if born before 1943) added to your future distribution amount. So in this case you would add four years—from age sixty-six (your NRA) to age seventy—of 8 percent compounded interest to your $2,000 baseline figure for a lifetime monthly check totaling $2,720. As you see, it can literally pay to wait.

Besides timing, taxes can affect the value of your Social Security distribution as well. If you and/or your spouse are still working and you elect to start taking benefits, then there's a good chance your Social Security check will be taxed. I refer to this as a "tax on a tax." It's not fair, it's not right, but it's reality. The government collects taxes for Social Security out of your paycheck over the span of your entire career; nevertheless, the Social Security check you receive in return will be taxed because it gets lumped together with your employment income. This can be avoided by deferring your distribution, yet millions of older working Americans continue getting taxed on their Social Security simply because they lack an understanding of how the system works. Bottom line: if you are employed and not in immediate need of supplemental income, then it rarely makes sense to start taking Social Security at this time.

Much like employment income, owning individual retirement accounts (IRAs) and other such savings vehicles can trigger a tax on your Social Security as well, even if you are no longer employed. This is an example of being penalized for being a good saver, especially when compared to those who didn't save much and are receiving similar Social Security checks tax free.

So Jeff, you're telling me the government will be taxing my Social Security check but not my neighbor's—that's no fair and makes no sense! Remember, it's the government we're talking about, so, no, it doesn't have to make sense, and yes, it's unfair. But as I often tell my kids, "Life's not fair!" Still, it's not reason enough to abandon taking responsibility for your own retirement savings by planning to live on Social Security income alone. I call that "planning to fail."

That's Social Security 101, a survey of the basics. The next step is finding a good financial planner (more on that in Chapter 18) who can help you navigate the system's more complex features and discern how to best use them to your advantage. "File and suspend" is one such facet to explore, along with those involving spousal benefits. If utilized properly, these features can substantially increase your total lifetime benefit. And while every Social Security situation is different, the primary objective remains the same— to maximize your overall benefit. Keep in mind, though, that this money should be just *part* of your total retirement income.

WE DON'T HAVE A PENSION PLAN AND IT DOESN'T LOOK LIKE SOCIAL SECURITY WILL BE ENOUGH—WHERE IS OUR MAIN SOURCE OF RETIREMENT FUNDING GOING TO COME FROM?

You guessed it: your hard-earned savings! This is where socking money away every paycheck—the *pay yourself first* principle—puts you on the path to financial independence.

Work retirement plans, such as a 401(k), 403(b), or 457, are the primary vehicles that most Americans use to reach this goal. These plans allow you to put money away on a pretax basis. The money grows in that account, tax deferred. What's more, some companies match a percentage of the money you contribute. With all the benefits these plans provide, you'd be foolish not to take advantage of them. Now, you can't start withdrawing those dollars until age fifty-nine and a half (I have no clue why the half is there), yet most people need to wait until at least sixty-five to be able to retire comfortably anyhow.

Interestingly, I've been setting up employer-sponsored retirement plans for decades, and without fail there are individuals who think twice about participating. They're often riding the excuse train: "I'm too young to think about retirement." "I can't save a dime." "Maybe next year will be a better time to start." Once I convince them to hop off and give this saving thing a try, they're usually the first ones in line to thank me later. They often report that having their contributions deducted directly out of their paycheck eased the "saving" transition to the point that they no longer noticed it anymore. Consequently their outlook for retirement one day has gotten a whole lot brighter.

If your employer does not offer a company retirement plan, then you need to investigate your individual retirement plan options. The most common two are the IRA and Roth IRA. They each have their own limitations (refer to the Glossary at the end of the book), but most Americans are eligible to contribute significant dollar amounts into these plans with loads of accompanying tax benefits.

If you are self-employed or have any independent-contractor income, then you are eligible for an SEP plan, which allows you put a sizeable amount of money away on a tax-deductible basis. Currently SEP plans allow you to contribute over $52,000 per year (IRAs and Roths are capped at $5,500). Again, refer to the Glossary at the end of the book for details.

What I hope you gleaned from this chapter is the following: retirement is a weighty, multifaceted issue that requires financial discipline coupled with a sound investment strategy in order to get you there. By deciding to save early and often, into any number of investment vehicles, you will arrive at your destination—*financial independence*—that much faster.

16

FINANCIAL INDEPENDENCE AT LAST! HOW DO WE MAKE A SMOOTH TRANSITION INTO RETIREMENT?

I'm a strong advocate for easing into retirement rather than going cold turkey—it's the approach that works best for most people, but of course there are exceptions.

Take my friend Sam, who was a high school teacher and cross-country coach for thirty-five years. He had a pension, and at age sixty-four he said, "I'm done." So he quit his job, took his pension, and was happy as a clam.

Conversely, his friend Jack was a sixty-seven-year-old engineer and client of mine. He worked ten-hour days on average and rarely took a vacation other than his allotted two weeks a year. During one of our review meetings Jack indicated he was thinking of retiring. He was ready to leave behind the long days at the office and the grind of a lengthy, traffic-laden commute. After a subsequent review of his overall plan I was able to share the fantastic news with him: he had finally achieved financial independence—retirement was definitely an option. A great big smile crossed Jack's face; in his mind I had just given him the green light to hang 'em up ASAP and start planning his trip around the world! As the voice of reason—part of my job description—I chimed in: "Do you think that's a good idea?"

"Why not?" he said. "Sam retired cold turkey, no problem."

"That's true," I said. "But Sam was a school teacher accustomed to lots of time off—holidays, weeklong breaks, three months in the summer . . ."

You see, Sam already knew how to occupy all that free time when he wasn't working. Jack, however, was a fifty-plus hours a week, fifty weeks a year kind of guy, and he had been ever since he started his career over four decades ago. How would he fill his days and nights, week after week, month after month? I'm not sure he really thought through how his wife, Susan, would feel about suddenly having him underfoot 24/7 either!

After further discussion I convinced Jack to talk things over with Susan first and make sure they were on the same page going forward. Next he needed to have a candid conversation with his employer about his impending retirement and come up with a game plan on how exactly that would play out.

Although his company was certainly happy for him, at the same time they were somewhat taken aback by Jack's retirement news. They didn't see it coming, and frankly, they didn't want to lose him. He was an exceptional engineer at the top of his field who possessed a very specialized skill set, one that would be hard to immediately replace.

So together they hammered out an agreement in which Jack would cut back to three days a week over the course of a few months. Then he'd transition into consulting and contracting jobs on an as-needed basis. This would give the company time to train or hire a replacement, and Jack would be able to get his "retirement" feet wet without jumping in hook, line, and sinker. Susan supported the arrangement as well; it was a win-win for all parties involved.

Jack continued taking on contracting jobs with his old firm for a few years. This allowed him to keep working in the field he loved, but he was able to do it on his terms. Meanwhile he was lining his pockets with some extra cash and filling time in his otherwise wide-open calendar. Eventually Jack stopped the contracting work altogether, and the transition into full-blown retirement was complete.

Looking back on it now, easing rather than diving into retirement was the wiser choice for their situation, as it is for most couples. Susan's house is her castle; Jack's sudden prolonged daily presence would have put forty-something years of marriage to the test, for sure. A gradual transition was just what the (financial) doctor ordered. Sure it took some settling in and getting used to, but when you've worked your whole lives to reach this point, you darn well better make the most of it once you get there! Now they spend time with their grandkids, enjoy traveling, and have even joined a bridge group. Although they each have their own interests, they happily spend time together at home as well.

Health insurance was a separate retirement-related matter Jack had to deal with. At the time Jack decided to retire he was sixty-seven, but his wife, Susan, was only sixty-three. He was on Medicare, but she wasn't—remember, you need to be sixty-five or older to qualify. Knowing this, Jack negotiated to keep Susan covered through his employer's health plan until she reached age sixty-five. If he hadn't, there would have been a two-year gap when Susan had no health care coverage. They could have utilized COBRA, a temporary extension policy, but that only lasts for eighteen months. Health insurance, as you've surely heard, isn't cheap. It would have cost them a fortune just to keep Susan insured. It's imperative that you not overlook the health insurance piece of the puzzle as you sort out your retirement strategy.

WHAT ELSE CAN WE DO TO SMOOTH THE TRANSITION TO RETIREMENT?

There are lots of creative ways to ease into retirement so you're not lonely or bored—or driving your spouse nuts—but are still making a modest income.

Roger, another teacher I know, ran a souvenir stand at Dodger Stadium as a side business while he taught high school full time. When he decided to retire from teaching, he opted to keep the side gig. This allowed him stay busy enough and put a little extra spending money in his pockets to boot.

My client Barbara recently retired from her hospital nursing position. Not long afterward she decided to take a job at a local crafts store teaching sewing lessons. She enjoys being around people with similar interests. It's a great way for her to ease into retirement, doing something she loves and getting paid to do it!

It should go without saying: your spouse *must* factor into the retirement equation for the sake of both your financial and marital happiness. Some employers offer early retirement packages, which sound *great*—who doesn't want to retire early?—but they need to be thoughtfully considered. *How will this affect your spouse? Will it affect your spouse's ability to retire? Will you still need your spouse's salary to survive?*

Another factor to consider before leaving the workforce altogether is your employer-sponsored retirement plan. Suppose you work for a public company and own company stock within your 401(k); it may not be in your best interest to cash out that stock at this time. There is a rather complicated planning technique known as net unrealized appreciation (NUA) that can be used to your advantage in such a situation. This strategy can result in a tremendous tax benefit for you in retirement; a good advisor will be familiar with NUA and know exactly how to implement it.

A few years back a couple came to me with the oft-asked retirement question—you guessed it!: Do we have enough money to retire comfortably? After reviewing their accounts I noticed that the wife had a large chunk of company stock in her 401(k). With careful planning, utilizing the NUA calculator, we were able to save the couple tens of thousands of dollars in taxes. If they had met with me *after* selling the company stock, the opportunity to save them big money would have been lost. NUA is one of those "Please, don't attempt to do this on your own" planning ideas. Getting your financial and tax advisors involved is critical to its success.

WHAT WILL WE DO WITH OUR TIME NOW THAT WE'RE NOT WORKING?

If you are in the early stages of mapping out your retirement, you need to have a goal. Figure out how much money you're going to need and what you want to do with it once you're no longer working. Planning and communication are key—you and your spouse want to be in control of the ship and, more importantly, to be certain you are both steering it in the same direction.

Couples spend more time planning their annual vacation than they do discussing what retirement looks like to them *as a couple*. This can be problematic, as people often have very different visions of retirement. Your bucket list might involve buying an Airstream travel trailer and barreling across the country, whereas your partner's may include wanting to spend more time with the grandkids. Or paint. Or go back to school. Or volunteer somewhere. The point is: you need to think about what retirement looks like to you and then discuss those ideas with your spouse.

When you retire there are pockets of time you need to consider as a couple: apart time and together time. In an ideal world you want to experience "symmetry" in your retirement life; that is, find a balance between the amount of time you spend together and the time you spend apart. An example might be: I hit golf balls while my wife does yoga. Or I play poker and she plays bridge with her girlfriends. Or I head out for a golfing weekend with my buddies and she heads to a spa weekend in Palm Springs. Those are things we do on our own, and that's great. But then there are things we do together. We love to go out to dinner, we love to travel, we're both interested in history, and we are both mildly obsessed with Hawaii. Finding the right balance is essential. It's also necessary. For over twenty years we've spent most of our days apart. It would be a challenge to spend 24/7 together. That's a tough transition for anyone to make.

I often advise retirees to find something they've always wanted to do and *go do it*. Can't ride a bike? Now's a good time to learn! Want to paint? Go buy some brushes and canvases and take a class. Ditto for yoga, Pilates, hiking, tennis, golf, bridge—whatever. But if those are things you do alone, make sure to come up with things you can do as a couple as well.

Kendra and I often talk about our future retirement. Luckily we both dream of spending more time together in Hawaii. It's a place near and dear to our hearts; we spend a week there together every year, and we'd love for it to be longer. So, for us, Hawaii represents a common pursuit. It inspires us to sock more money away because we've got an emotional goal we want to fulfill.

WHAT HAPPENS IF ONE RETIRES AND THE OTHER DOESN'T?

Ah, yes, lopsided life phases. It happens. Just because you're married doesn't mean you're at the same place in your careers. Although you may be ready to focus on your flute playing, your husband might still want to head to the office every day. That's okay. Sometimes people aren't quite ready to give up working yet.

Other times they just want a few more Benjamins in the bank. I stated this earlier, but it bears repeating: if you are not yet eligible for Medicare, then staying on the job can provide much-needed health benefits. You don't want your financial house to crumble on account of health care costs. God forbid something were to happen to you and you didn't have proper health insurance coverage—you could be financially ruined.

Note about compatibility: If you're not working and your partner still is, it's your job to pick up the slack around the house. Take the vacuum out for a spin! Make the beds! Have dinner waiting on the table! Otherwise, you might have an unhappy, tired spouse at the end of the day, and that's no fun for anyone. Handle the honey-do's with a smile.

There are a great many things to think about and discuss as a couple before you retire. Whether you're financially independent or still working toward that day, this should be an exciting chapter in your life. For those couples who have already reached this pinnacle, your commitment to organizing a solid game plan and seeing it through has put you in a position many Americans only dream about.

17

WHAT'S ESTATE PLANNING ALL ABOUT?

Many pages ago, in Chapter 14, we talked about what life should look like when you hit the jackpot, maybe in the form of an inheritance. I'm going to turn it around on you: What about when you are providing the jackpot?

Here's a sad but true fact: we are not immortal. Not me, not you—none of us. I say this with 100 percent certitude. The end is inevitable. Someday.

The great tragedy, of course, is that none of us knows exactly when our last day will come. People are certainly living longer than they used to. One day, I believe, it will be completely normal to live in a world filled with centenarians.

But individually you and I don't know our expiration date. Will we leave enough to make our kids rich, or will we spend our last dollar as we draw our last breath? My attorney jokingly tells clients to choose cremation and let the check to the funeral home bounce.

All joking aside, this is not fun to talk about; it's one of the most emotionally taxing conversations I have with my clients.

Likewise, it is one of the most procrastinated activities in life—along with making a budget! Although it's scary and intimidating, it's also essential. In my home state of California, dying unprepared can literally take hundreds of thousands of dollars out of whatever jackpot you leave.

But estate planning isn't just for death; it's for life too.[22] What if something happens to you—a car crash, a stroke—and you can't make decisions for yourself anymore?

I have a client named Ruth who runs a small business (think of your household as a business for a moment). A few years back she had a major heart attack. Thankfully, she survived. Prior to working with us, Ruth had no estate plan in place. While she was recovering from her heart attack the business had to close. Why? She had put no directives on how to run the business in her absence. It wasn't that the employees couldn't run it without her; it was they had nothing written in advance. Nobody knew how to pay the bills or access the bank account to pay the employees. There was zero contingency plan in place.

It took a year for Ruth to fully recover from her heart attack, and the business was closed down for the duration. Luckily, once she was finally able to open her doors again, despite twelve months of no revenue, the employees and customers faithfully returned. Would your business or household survive a scenario like this? Most can't.

This problem could be solved with proper planning. Somebody needs to have the power to pay your bills—it should be a person of your choosing stated clearly in your estate planning documents. Ideally this person would be local, but it's far more important to involve someone responsible, whom you trust, rather than someone in your backyard but with whom you are not comfortable.

Most people don't think they have enough money to even warrant a discussion about estate planning; they believe it's better suited for the Rockefellers and the Vanderbilts. To the contrary, it's suited for anyone who cares where their assets go after they die. Because no matter how little you have (or think you have), if you don't have an estate plan in place, the government will be more than happy to direct your money as they see fit. Personally I'd rather pass my estate into the hands of loved ones than into the hands of some bureaucrat!

At my office estate planning goes hand in hand with financial planning. Not doing an estate plan is like peanut butter without jelly. Both are good on their own, but they're that much tastier when combined. So my clients must create an estate plan when they work with me. It makes my job as their advisor much easier if—or when—they die or become incapacitated, and, of course, it's much better for them and their families.

A client of mine, a gentleman named Mr. Greene—yes, he has a first name, Bruce, but I've never actually used it—is just one of those people who commands respect. He's a former Marine who still wears his hair in a tight crew cut. His mother, who was also my client, died a few years back, at which time we met to review her estate. Everything was in impeccable order; all of her papers were perfectly arranged. Before she even hired me she had seen a competent attorney who had helped her write her estate plan.

As we were finishing up our meeting he became emotional. I saw his eyes glistening. Even though his mother had just peacefully died, knowing him as I did, I was taken aback by his display of emotion. Before I could say anything he looked me right in the eye and said, "Is it going to be this easy when I go?"

"What do you mean?" I asked.

"Well, everything you set up for my mother has worked," he said. "I want to make sure it will be this smooth for my kids. I don't want to be a burden on them." He was so grateful to his mother for her thoughtful planning. She wasn't a wealthy woman, but she really wanted to alleviate the stress of dealing with her estate when she died. His comments really moved me, especially when I realized it was coming from a place of appreciation and relief. I felt satisfied knowing I was able make his life a little easier during a time of great sorrow.

WHEN SHOULD WE START ESTATE PLANNING?

People tend to get serious about estate planning only after they have kids or after they experience a medical emergency. There's nothing like a heart attack to spur one into action! Then again, we tend to become very emotional during a health scare and may not always make the best decisions.

The onset of retirement can also awaken the need for some proper estate planning work. Facing their golden years, people come to the realization that life doesn't last forever, so they want to make sure their hard-earned cash gets directed where they want it to go.

A second marriage also causes people to act, especially if one spouse has kids from a prior marriage. They usually want to make certain those offspring receive an inheritance. If your second spouse outlives you and you do not have a proper estate plan, *they* are in control of your estate. It's then their choice whether to pass the money on to your kids or to keep it and shack up with the tennis pro—either would be perfectly legal. Yes, this does happen all too often, and yes, it can be easily prevented with some good estate planning.

If none of the aforementioned life events has gotten the estate planning ball rolling for you, then a good time to start would be *now*—not tomorrow, not when you've finished your "other" planning but in concurrence with your "other" planning. Remember, estate planning, along with life insurance and tax planning, make up the roof of your financial house. It's much-needed protection for your family in a world full of uncertainty.

When I discuss estate planning with clients, these are the mindsets I encounter:

The "do nothing." These people are somewhat selfish. They don't want to think about death, so they bury their heads in the sand and have put nothing in order.

The "do a little." These folks are aware they need to have some kind of estate plan in place, so they take baby steps. Maybe they write a will or type one out online. They don't do a trust, however, and that's a problem. (A will says where your stuff is going to go; a trust actually gets it there.) Wills alone are costly and contestable; it just takes one angry sibling for it to become a mess.

The "do a little more." These people find themselves in a bad situation, so they spring into (slight) action. They don't hire a professional, but they make a durable health care power of attorney, which is required in hospitals to make decisions on behalf of a loved one. Maybe they even create a financial durable power of attorney, but they do nothing else.

The "get 'er done." They want to have control while they are above ground, so they take my advice and hire a proper estate planner.

My advice: get 'er done! Here are some of the reasons why.

Let's start with your duty as a parent. You bring these children into the world, these little beings who rely on you to nurture them, teach them, and be there for them at all times. What happens if, God forbid, you and your spouse are in a tragic accident on the way home from date night? Or in a plane crash? These questions alone should inspire you to take estate planning action.

Kendra and I don't want some boilerplate state laws dictating what would happen to our kids in the event of our untimely deaths. But if we don't put our intentions in a plan, then the state will be more than happy to step in. These discussions can be gut wrenching, but I firmly believe it's best for you as a couple to do it rather than rely on your family to try to figure it out if something tragic happens to the two of you. Emotions will already be running high, and I've seen even the most well-intentioned families make poor decisions during these times.

What about the burden you place on your adult children? What if they have to fight with each other for authority and try to figure out what you wanted, all because you wouldn't take the time to put it in writing?

You can easily find a good estate planner through professional or personal references. If you already have an advisor or an accountant, they should know someone, as should business associates. Another option would be to seek a referral from a trusted friend. During your initial meetings with an estate-planning attorney make sure you are clear about your intentions as a couple. This person is drafting documents that are extremely important as you move forward in life, so it's crucial you hire someone you like and trust.

You can do it poorly by going online and filling out some documents then call it a day, or you can do it well by hiring a good estate attorney. It's up to you.

I'm pretty sure you know where I stand on the matter, but in case you don't: I vote for the expert. They'll make the whole process easier for you. A professional has seen all sorts of situations. They'll be thinking about the things you've never considered, asking you questions you never knew needed to be answered. What's more, creating an estate plan helps get you organized; it serves as a basis for your statement of assets, a moment in time when you look at *everything* as it is now and also think about what it will be in the future.

At the end of the day, good estate planning is about emptying your coffers to whomever or whatever you care about most. (I know it's not the IRS!)

WHY DO A LIVING TRUST?

For most of my clients, *get 'er done* means drafting a living trust. The really good thing about a living trust is that it's a flexible, fluid document. You can make changes to it if necessary just by adding an amendment to your document. So, say you chose to give your inheritance to your kids and later on decide you'd rather give it to your school or church or synagogue—that's fine. You can change your mind any time you want as long as you are alive and coherent.

Another important consideration: a living trust is a private document, unlike the probate process, which is a public forum that displays your assets (or liabilities) for all the world to see. The last thing you need is for your emotionally vulnerable heirs to be bombarded with requests for loans from friends or for offers to make a quick buck that are poor investments either which way!

This leads me to the next benefit of a living trust: you can decide what's required in order for family members to inherit your money; as in, they need to have graduated college or be twenty-five years of age or working in a certain career—what have you. You add the rules and stipulations, and if they don't adhere to them, well, then, they don't get the money. End of story.

It's true that a will can do most of these things. But not without minor or major court involvement, which will cost everyone a large amount of time and will only give lawyers and the government more of your money.

This brings me to a very important living trust function that a will cannot accomplish: probate avoidance. In many states the probate process, whereby the court is involved in administering the will, is incredibly expensive, even for relatively small estates. Such was the case for a client of mine whose mother had nothing more than a $500,000 condominium to her name when she died. It took eighteen months and $32,000 in expenses before my client and his brother could inherit the real estate. All of this could have been easily avoided with a good living trust. Not every state will be as expensive and time consuming as California, but some states are worse! Even in states that are less greedy, a living trust will save families significant money and anguish.

A DIFFERENT ASPECT OF ESTATE PLANNING—GIFTING!

Some wealthy people like to hoard their money, but I don't think that's smart. You can't take it with you when that fateful day arrives. I think it's wiser to gift money to people while you're still alive, for a variety of reasons. For starters, you can gift up to $14,000 a year to any one person while you're still alive without paying gift tax. By doing this on an annual basis you're shrinking the value of your estate and possibly avoiding estate taxes in the future. Incidentally, you don't need to disclose why you're doing it, but most of my clients who gift money to family benefit from getting to see what those individuals do with it.

Some recipients put it in the bank, some invest it, and still others blow it all at a shopping mall. Based on their behavior, you can decide what kinds of rules are needed before you bequeath money to them. Remember my client, Doris, whose four kids each blew through their $100,000 inheritance within six months? You can bet she would have instructed some oversight of her hard-earned dollars had she known how they would handle it.

You can also opt to create a school scholarship or have a building named after you. Personally, I have other plans. A friend who I played college baseball with died tragically not long ago. My goal is to rebuild our campus field and get the university to rename it in his honor. That seems like a good way to gift my money.

And you may recall our earlier college planning discussion whereby grandparents can gift money to help fund their grandkids' education. You rack up some major warm fuzzy good feelings by doing so. It's heartening to know that you are responsible for someone's advancement in life and, even better, that you are still around to witness it. I have many grandparent clients who've proudly watched their grandchild walk across the stage to receive their degree. They take great satisfaction knowing that they made that walk possible without oodles of student loan debt.

HOW DO WE MAKE SURE OUR KIDS HAVE ACCESS TO OUR ACCOUNTS IN THE EVENT OF A MEDICAL CRISIS?

You must have an electronic storage (I even have clients use a thumb drive) or a fireproof safe where you keep all of your important information: passwords, codes, copies of your estate-planning documents, professionals to contact, and so forth. In addition, this must include a list of your current doctors, their contact information, and an updated list of medications you are taking, along with copies of health care documents, in particular a health care directive and durable power of attorney. This needs to be extremely secure yet available to the people you put in charge if you were incapacitated for an extended period of time.

You should also keep a budget and data on your income and expenses. This information should be updated regularly. Your family must be able to track down all of your accounts along with the advisors to call. It is also helpful to have updated medical information in case you end up in the emergency room. Nobody likes to think about or plan for these things, but remember what Mr. Greene said: "I want to make sure it will be this easy for my kids. I don't want to be a burden on them." All this extra planning, to go along with your formal estate plan, can really help your family during a time of extreme emotional distress.

An update on Ruth, my client who survived her heart attack. Recently she went back into the hospital with another illness and has been out of commission for a few months. This time the business stayed open and is running like a well-oiled machine. Why? You guessed it—she whipped up a proper plan with contingencies. Her decision makers knew where all the day-to-day information was kept; the documents allowed them access and authority. The business is paying its bills and collecting revenue, which means she has money coming in while she recovers. What a difference a little planning makes.

18

HOW DO WE FIND AND HIRE
A FINANCIAL ADVISOR?

First things first: many couples think they can deal with their finances all on their own. They don't see a need for people like me because, in their opinion, I'm just an unnecessary added expense.

You *can* do it yourself—in theory. There's lots of information in this book to keep you on the right track and tons of websites that are dedicated to this stuff too.

But there are a few things you need to ask yourself before you can determine whether you need outside assistance. For example:

Do you like this kind of work?

Do you have the time to do it yourself, or would you be better served focusing on other aspects of your life?

Do you have the skill set to formulate a game plan (i.e., financial house) for success and then maintain it? And can you continually review and update your plan so as to stay on track?

Because you are actually reading this book, I would say the most important questions of all are these:

Are you able to manage your spouse's emotions and expectations of the game plan along with your own?
Will you keep yourself and your spouse accountable to the plan without getting into arguments?
Will going about it on your own cause you, as a couple, mountains of stress?

You really need to think long and hard about each one of these questions. Because yes, you're right: financial advisors are an added expense. But I would argue that we are necessary elements to a happy financial life—and a harmonious relationship. We can guide you and keep you on the right path. As I said way back in the beginning of this book: I'm not just a money guy; I often play couple's therapist, counselor, and mediator. And I know quite well just how difficult this can be.

Here are some other reasons why people don't seek out a good advisor:

1. They think they don't have enough money. Okay, I'll admit that our industry definitely markets to the affluent. That's often our target audience, which I think is a big mistake. Middle America, the oft-neglected group when it comes to financial discussions, are the people who need our help the most. I'm proud to say that I built a very successful practice helping middle-class Americans.

At my company, Trilogy, we focus on two important factors when assessing clients: the "A" score and the "M" score. The "A" score refers to the clients' *ability* to build a successful plan. This includes net worth, household income, future earnings potential—your basic, everyday financial stuff. Most traditional firms use this kind of approach, but they stop there. And that's a shame, because the "M" score is critical. "M" stands for the couples' *motivation* to build a successful game plan.

Generally advisors want people with both high A and M scores, but our firm is far more focused on the M factor. It's not that we work pro bono—advisors need to earn a living—but we are looking for couples who want to build a plan and stick to it. I often say in company meetings, "I don't care if a couple has a net worth of eight dollars or eight figures—it's far more important that they have the motivation to succeed!" I want to work with couples who *want* to get their financial house in order, period.

2. They are too busy or don't have enough time. *Really?* How can that be? You've invested time and energy in reading this book, yet you're really too busy to find a financial advisor? Did you know that people spend more time watching reruns of their favorite old shows (mine was *Gilligan's Island*) than they do building their financial house? Let me tell you something: procrastination— short-term pleasure with long-term pain—is *not* a strategy for success. So put down the remote and take the time to find a qualified advisor who will get you off Procrastination Street and on to creating a sound financial game plan.

Incidentally, does Gilligan ever get off that island? I keep hearing about people on TV getting kicked off the island each week, but I've just been *too busy* helping my clients to find out.

3. They are too afraid to look because they might see the reality of their situation. These couples have buried their heads in the sand—an escape from reality, the old "what we don't know can't hurt us" philosophy. Again, this is not an attitude that puts them on the fast track to financial freedom. These people simply don't want to know how they're fairing financially. Or, at the least, they don't want to think about it. Arguably this is the toughest behavior to deal with. If this sounds like you and your spouse, use the quiz and this book as catalysts to *change*!

4. They are interested in hiring an advisor but are just not sure how to go about finding one they trust. Start by tapping into your existing personal relationships—friends, relatives, neighbors, church members . . . people you trust who can introduce you to professionals they trust. As an advisor, I believe that good, sound planning derives from the trusted relationship I develop with *both* my clients, as a couple. You will be obliged to share the innermost financial details of your life together in order to design an effective game plan, so it's imperative you work with someone you both trust implicitly.

If you are the first couple amongst your friends and family to seek out an advisor, then you should turn to your other professional relationships. We founded Trilogy with an emphasis on helping people understand the complexities of financial, tax, and estate planning and how they interact. Who does your tax return—a CPA? Can they recommend someone who might be a good fit? What about your estate planner or lawyer? Can they recommend a trusted professional advisor? I'm betting they can.

WHAT DO WE NEED
FROM AN ADVISOR?

In a sentence, someone with whom you can be completely transparent. Plans can't be built without full disclosure, and I require it. My initial interview with clients, which I call the "Discovery Meeting," lasts about one and a half hours. It's very upfront and open on both sides. I ask a ton of questions, and then I spend most of my time listening and taking notes (hence, my feeling like I'm a therapist). Instead of analyzing bank and investment statements (hopefully not credit card statements!) or dissecting numbers, we review their War of the Wallets Quiz. I ask them about their important goals, their dreams, what they hope to accomplish.

We spend time discussing:

Their past: How did they get where they are? What sorts of mistakes did they make? What do they wish they had done differently? What has gone well?

The present: What brought them here today? Is there something they are trying to change or achieve? What does the future look like to them? What types of things do they wish they had?

The future: What do they aspire to as a couple? What does their life look like in five years? Ten years? And here's a question I ask every couple in our first meeting together: If we were sitting here X years from today, what would have needed to happen for them personally to consider our relationship successful?

That first meeting is, quite frankly, the most important one for both the couple and me. When it's all said and done I need to feel confident that I can help them reach their goals and they need to feel secure that I'm the guy to help them do just that. Translation: I need to like them, and they need to like me. If as a couple you don't have that gut feeling, then it's not the right fit. That's okay. Just move on and interview someone else.

It's the advisor's job to help the client make prudent decisions and organize their finances in a way that will prepare them for the predictably unpredictable moments in life. When life takes its unimaginable turns, you will have a plan in place and an advisor to lean on for guidance, financially and emotionally.

HOW DO WE INTERVIEW AN ADVISOR?

After reading this book and completing the War of the Wallets Quiz you should have a better understanding of where you are in your financial compatibility journey and how far along you are on the road to financial independence—if you're even on it at all. Armed with this knowledge, you can embark upon your mission of finding a trusted advisor.

During the interview process, if you feel an advisor is immediately trying to sell you something or not listening to you, then you should *run*, not walk, out the door! At the initial meeting I never discuss products or markets. That comes after you find a good— that is, compatible—fit. The emphasis should be on good rapport and good planning.

If the advisor is not asking intelligent questions that are applicable to both of you, then they're not for you. Sometimes I'll ask couples who've been my clients for a year or so why they chose to work with me. I remember one couple in particular, Andy and Laura, who'd had many advisors over the years. When I posed that question to them their response really stuck with me. "You asked us questions that nobody had ever asked us in a financial meeting," they both said. "Topics that really mattered to us—Have we started saving for our daughter's wedding? Do we really like being a landlord of our rental properties? How are we were going to handle my ailing mother?"

Good advisors ask good questions and listen intently to your answers. Bottom line: *they care*! Don't work with anyone who doesn't.

Take the time together to prepare a list of questions you'd like to ask the advisor; share your concerns, goals, dreams, and aspirations with them. After all, when you go to see a doctor and he comes into the exam room (twenty-five or thirty minutes late) and asks, "Where does it hurt?" you don't say, "You're the doctor! *You* figure it out!!"

After you are comfortable with the relationship and are confident you can build a game plan together, then you need to discuss . . .

HOW SHOULD WE PAY OUR ADVISOR—WITH A COMMISSION OR FEES?

If your mother somehow forgot to mention this growing up: "Nothing in life is free." So when you find a good fit with an advisor you can expect to pay for their service. Earlier I mentioned that I believe good advisors will help anyone who is motivated to build a game plan, no matter their net worth. If you have a low net worth, an advisor might recommend a commission over a fee for service. And that's completely acceptable. Because you're just getting started and don't have a lot of money, your plan should be simple and straightforward.

As you progress in life and things become more complicated, you're going to need a more formal written game plan with periodic reviews and updates from your trusted advisor. At this point paying a fee for service or a fee to manage your assets usually makes the most sense. But remember that the most important part of paying your advisor is understanding how and what you are paying for.

WHERE SHOULD WE INVEST OUR MONEY TO REACH OUR GAME PLAN GOALS?

So you've found yourself a trusted advisor whom you are willing to pay for their services—job well done! Now what? A good place to start would be filling out your budget worksheet and reviewing the financial house diagram located at the back of the book. You can also go to www.jeffmotske.com and print copies of each to work off of from home.

Once you've met with your advisor to review your information and designed a plan together, you must make sure it gets properly funded so as to achieve your goals. This involves "running the numbers." Where, what, and how much you invest depends on many factors; time, risk, and education are critical measurements. Think back to the compatibility quiz—there were questions on risk. How did you answer those individually? How did you answer those as a couple? How soon do you need the money for your goals? Can you sleep at night, or are you awake at all hours worried about your investment portfolio (Sleep Test)?

Another critical question is: Do you as a couple understand what you own? A good advisor will sit down and explain everything you own in your plan until you understand it and are comfortable with how it works. Do not be satisfied with anyone who says, "Trust me . . . " or "Put your money with us, and we'll take care of the rest." That's not good enough.

WHAT SHOULD WE EXPECT FROM AN ADVISOR?

In a sentence? You should expect independent and objective advice that collaborates with your other trusted advisors and provides good service en route to ultimately reaching your goals.

Let's unpack that sentence:

Independent. This means the advisor has no "hidden agenda" or loyalty to one investment over another. The advisor is unbiased in their recommendations, and they truly have your best interests at heart. They only place you in company-specific products when it makes the best sense for you. No one company is the best at everything; an independent advisor has the flexibility to pick and choose the best investment options available to fund your game plan.

Objective. A good advisor looks at the big picture. He helps manage the emotional aspects of investing and planning. I often say that part of my role is to take the emotions out of investing. When the market falls off a cliff I allay panic; when it shoots into the stratosphere I hang on to my client's ankles and keep their feet near the ground. This way couples stay on track so they can reach their dreams and goals. And yep, I sometimes play referee in those difficult decisions between spouses. To do so I *must* be objective.

Service. This should be a no-brainer. When you need something, how quickly do they respond? Are your questions getting answered? Does your advisor have a courteous and competent team? Does your advisor have a contingency plan in case they get ill?

Professional collaboration. Do all of your trusted advisors— financial, tax, estate—know each other and work together on your behalf? I started Trilogy back in 1999 on this simple yet crucial concept. It has become more common in our industry, but it's still not commonplace. You want this collaboration among your advisors. If it's not a facet of your current situation, start by simply introducing your trusted advisors to one another. Explain to them that they're all part of your team, and the goal is for everyone to work together so the two of you can reach your financial goals. If they are not willing to have a professional conversation about coordinating efforts on your behalf, then I would move on. The deeper into the game plan you go, the more critical this becomes.

If you've read this far, you probably figured out by now that I don't earn my living as a writer! Naturally I'm going to recommend a financial advisor for most people. That being said, if you think long and hard about the questions I raised at the beginning of this chapter, many of you will recognize the value that an independent, objective advisor brings to the process of building your financial house. Think of an advisor as your general contractor. Sure, you can build a house without one, but do you have the time to coordinate all the moving parts and the know-how to make certain that it's being constructed properly? If you don't, put that responsibility in the hands of someone who does.

19

FINANCIAL SUCCESS STORIES DEFINED BY YOU AS A COUPLE

Everyone has a different opinion of success. What's yours?

To me, financial success has been reached the day work becomes an option, not a necessity. When work becomes an option, you've gained financial freedom. Financial freedom creates more opportunities to pursue your personal mission statement. Part of my personal mission statement is to do something wonderful for someone else every single day. That might have nothing to do with finances and could be something simple like smiling at a stranger in the elevator or complimenting them on something they're wearing. Or it could be something big, like writing a check to an organization that needs help. Or volunteering my time in the community. The more financial freedom I have, the easier it is to fulfill my personal mission statement.

My personal mission statement led me to write this book. There were many days when the hard work I put into it constituted my "something wonderful for someone" that day—and hopefully that someone is you! Helping people aspire to financial independence and hearing their stories when they achieve it bring me great satisfaction and motivate me to work even harder. When couples get organized, build a plan, and commit to it, I can see their bright financial future, and this brings me joy. This is my opinion of success.

The point is that everyone defines success differently, and that's perfectly okay. The bigger issue is whether, at the end of a day, you can say it was a successful one by your own definition. Each day on the way home from work I ask myself: Was today a success? Did I accomplish what I set out to do? I rarely take a phone call during my drive home, which is all of about ten minutes, so I have time to ponder these questions.

What questions should you be asking yourself and discussing with your spouse?

What goals should you be setting? Where do we start?

The way I see it, you must undertake a set of five core strategies to reach financial independence. You need to embrace them, and if that requires *change*, then commit to the change.

1. Create a written game plan (financial house) with a fully transparent budget you both can live by.
2. Eliminate *all* bad debt (and keep it from coming back).
3. Fully fund your 911 Fund, which proves you're living within your means.
4. Pay yourselves first by saving at least 15 percent or more of your gross income.
5. Communicate with each other on a regular basis. Commit to Financial Date Nights during which you review and revise your game plan and make smart financial decisions together.

This should include celebrating your successes along the way! Have mini-celebrations. For example, when you pay off your bad debt, go out and treat each other to something special. (Just don't rack up more bad debt doing so!) Make sure the celebrations are proportional to the effort required to attain the particular goal you are celebrating.

Also, make sure you plan something particularly great for the day when you achieve financial independence. And once you have attained your financial freedom, don't stop there; consider setting up legacy and/or charitable endeavors—when life gives you options, choose to make a difference every step of the way.

As I've shown you throughout this book it *is* possible to get out of debt, create wealth, and live within your means. Working together makes the road smoother and increases the likelihood you'll reach your goals that much sooner. I know. I've *seen* it.

Here are some of my favorite success stories from people who came to see me in a state of uncertainty as to whether they would ever reach their financial goals . . . and emerged triumphantly.

ROB AND SHANNON BUY THEIR DREAM HOME (CREATE A PLAN)

Rob and Shannon are the sort of people I love to work with—a young motivated couple. But they were in a very bad situation.

The good news: Shannon was pregnant. The bad news: they lived in a second-floor condo that also happened to be "upside-down" . . . not the second floor—the condo value! (As you may recall, that means they owed more on the condo than it was worth.) The surprise: they hadn't planned on starting a family this quickly. The double surprise: they were having twins!

Their condo was simply no place to raise two small children. Although they had already been saving toward a new house, they couldn't walk away from the condo without damaging their credit, so how exactly were they going to buy their "dream house," the "right" house to raise their new family?

We sat down together and went over their options. As always, first I asked about their dreams and goals, and that's when they told me they wanted to buy a house appropriate for their family. Their dream home was not some mansion with marble floors but rather a single-story house with room for everyone.

We went over their budget. They could afford the down payment by the time the babies arrived, but they'd need to substantially change their lifestyle in order to accelerate their savings rate. They benefited from a promotion for Rob and a slight uptick in the real estate market. We set aside some money to help turn the condo right side up, so Rob and Shannon were able to sell it for the amount they needed to pay off the loan. By sticking to the plan, they saved enough for the down payment on their dream home and moved in just before the babies were born. The twins never had to live in the condo; instead, today they have their own rooms and a yard to burn off all their excess energy.

LISA AND SCOTT REIN IN THE SPENDING (ELIMINATE BAD DEBT)

Let's shift gears to the newlyweds! I started working with Lisa and Scott about ten years ago. When I first met with them they were recently married with a fair amount of debt. They both had nice jobs, but they liked to live it up a little. In particular, they loved to travel. Sometimes they'd get their credit card bill and say, "Oh well! We'll just pay the minimum this month." Before they knew it they were in five figures of credit card debt. They had good jobs with plenty of income, but they were just spending too much and did not want to sacrifice today for the future. But they realized they were digging a hole that might be too big for them to climb out of. That's when they reached out to me.

After several candid meetings we discussed what needed to change in order to put them on the path to financial independence.

I insisted they make *and* follow an agreed-upon budget. They didn't want to, but they understood they had to.

With some hard work and effective communication, we created a budget, and Lisa and Scott managed to stick to it! Some years later they confided in me that they actually feel their budget gives them more freedom. Imagine that! They know how much they can spend and still abide by the plan. They have since earned significant raises at work, were able to pay off the credit card debt, and are socking away money for college for their two young children. They own most of their home (the bank still owns a little), and they have solid retirement savings built into their game plan. Lisa and Scott still love to travel, but they're far more mindful of what they spend (having to buy four plane tickets instead of two will have that effect). I'm confident that if they stay the course, they'll see many happy days ahead.

ELAINE STARTS FROM SCRATCH AT SIXTY-ONE (BUDGETING AND SPENDING)

Elaine came to me five years ago just after her husband died in a freak accident. She was sixty-one at the time and still dealing with the emotional scars of her loss. She was also carrying the burden of not knowing how to manage her money. Her late husband had taken care of all the finances—bills, investments, insurance, and so on. He made a budget but never explained anything to his wife and kept her on a tight financial leash. Elaine and I needed to start from scratch on the educational part of planning. She had never touched the checkbook and literally had not written a check in over a decade! She needed to learn how to manage the checkbook, pay the bills, and make sure the deposits got recorded.

After our initial discovery meeting and several organizational reviews, we set up a budget. I educated her on her finances and put a plan in place so she could stay retired. Elaine was doing well early on, but that didn't last for long, as she soon began spending beyond her budget. I understood her behavior; this was the first time she ever had the financial freedom to spend. Elaine was living beyond her means, and her husband was no longer there to rein her in.

Note to younger readers: If the spending leash is too restrictive, you are going to create friction in your relationship someday, if you aren't already, which could lead to outrageous spending in the future. Sit down and work out a budget with a sensible spending plan that includes his, hers, and ours.

Because Elaine could not stay on budget, we had to review where her nondiscretionary dollars were going. It turns out she was spending on family and friends, picking up everyone's meal tab and taking her family on trips for which she was paying the lion's share of the expense. I explained to her that she could not afford to keep this up or else she would be living with her kids, so she quickly wised up and has been far more cautious with her spending. Elaine has turned the corner and put the guardrails back up. This has allowed her to stay retired and to enjoy her family without having to move in with them! It took a tutorial on budgeting and spending—and a wee bit of a learning curve—for her to finally see the light.

RON AND PATTI FIND A WAY
(*TOGETHER* GOAL)

My clients, Ron and Patti, are a married couple in their early fifties who own and operate a manufacturing firm. I have visited their place of business many times; they have a great operation that turns a nice profit annually. Prior to one of our review meetings I had concluded that, as a couple, they could save a boatload of money in taxes by maxing out Patti's 401(k) contribution each year. What's more, this would push additional dollars toward their retirement savings—the number-one goal on their priority list.

I presented this idea on two separate occasions, and each time it went over like a turd in a punchbowl. What was I missing? It was a "no brainer" from a tax and retirement planning perspective. Come to find out that Patti used a substantial portion of her paycheck for her own spending money, and if we put the maximum allowed into her 401(k), she would be left with fewer dollars to spend—in her mind, she was getting a pay cut. An easy solution would have been for Ron to give Patti a larger paycheck to offset the difference. But he didn't want any part of that idea either. Ron was concerned that his long-term employees would take a harsh view of him giving his wife a substantial raise. I could see the logic. But the two were at an impasse, and tensions were beginning to mount.

I set to work diffusing the situation in our very next meeting. First, I reminded them that retirement was their primary, foremost, top banana, numero-uno goal and that the three of us should be working as a team to reach it. Next, I explained that it doesn't really matter whose name is on the retirement account if they are planning for retirement *together*. Once I was able to assuage their emotions, they were then able to see the financial wisdom in my advice. They agreed that Patti should fully fund her 401(k) and that they'd set aside spending money for her from other joint accounts to make up the difference.

We found a way, and consequently, they are well on their way to financial independence.

SAM AND ELLEN CAN RETIRE (HALLELUJAH!)

Sam built a successful career in the media business. He grew up very poor in the South, which shaped him into the kindhearted, humble man he is today. The more notoriety and fame he gained, the more he turned to helping others. His wife, Ellen, had worked in education all her life, and although teaching is a very noble profession—here's to two of my sisters who are teachers!—I think we can all agree that it's not especially lucrative.

When I started working with Sam and Ellen three years ago they were incredibly good savers, but they were concerned about being able to sustain their current lifestyle through their retirement years. Sam was more of a risk taker, whereas Ellen was very conservative. Sam had a high degree of trust in people, whereas Ellen was far more guarded. Some of their most urgent questions for me during our initial meeting included: How are we doing? Do we have enough to maintain our lifestyle in retirement? Are we taking too much risk or not enough? Can we be more charitable?

After gathering and then reviewing all of their information— they had accounts everywhere—I came to the conclusion that what they really needed was an organized game plan. Once that was in place they would be able to have confidence in their ability to fully retire comfortably. We addressed their varying risk tolerances and ended up "reeling" Sam in a little, but we also discussed the need for growth in their portfolio. We spent a lot of time getting to know each other; they easily met my criteria for taking on a new client. I liked them, and it was apparent that they liked my ideas and me personally. At the conclusion of our second meeting Sam and Ellen were comfortable moving forward with the plan we drew up.

In our most recent review session I let them know they had achieved my definition of financial success. Work was now an option, not a requirement to survive, and joy was written all over their faces. Not long afterward Sam stopped working and devoted more time to his philanthropic interests. He is the emcee at many charitable functions and loves helping in the community.

Ellen, however, continues to love her work in education. In fact, she is celebrating her fiftieth year in that field—right on! (I think she must have started her career at age twelve). She wakes up every day choosing to go to school and help kids learn. I have witnessed her in action, and it's incredible to see her passion pour out on campus. It's even more profound knowing that she is doing this because she *wants* to, not because she must.

Why are they financially successful? They were already practicing the four core strategies; they just needed help putting it all together and fine tuning number five: communication and assurance. If I didn't help them with number five, then they would still be wondering:

- Do we have enough?
- Can we be more charitable?
- Are we taking too much risk or not enough?

To wrap things up, a quick tip guide for financial success:

Plan

The first step is the hardest one—it gets better after that. Change isn't always easy, but it's necessary.

Communicate

If you're the talker in the relationship, start listening more. If you're the listener in the relationship, start talking more.

Change

Change is a key ingredient to continued success—not just in money but also in life.

If you don't like the path you're traveling on or see trouble ahead, then you need to *change* your course!

Get Real

Be open, honest, and transparent with each other.

Get Smart

Take what you have learned in this book and act on it.
     And remember: *nobody plans to fail—they fail to plan!*

EPILOGUE

Writing this book has been an incredible venture, one I have taken great pleasure in along the way. I am grateful you have allowed me to share my knowledge with you in hopes that it will positively affect your relationship. My wish is that you will enjoy a happy, loving marriage, one free from financial angst and argument.

I wrote this book with the intention that you could pick it up at any point in your life and benefit from the information provided on a myriad of topics. When money issues arise in the future—and they will—use this guide to keep your financial house prospering.

You *can* stay in control of your financial future. I don't want you as a couple to need to rely on anyone else for your financial well-being. Work as a team so that money becomes a source of financial freedom instead of conflict.

The fundamentals don't change, even if you need to change to embrace them! No matter where you are on your journey, there are some core principles to live by:

1. Create a game plan together (build your financial house).

2. Establish a budget (be fully transparent while attacking any bad debt).
3. Live within your means (pay yourselves first).
4. Communicate (be a financial team).
5. Aspire to financial independence.

Put the book down and start today. Establish a Financial Date Night. Agree to embrace these core principles together. Work together and motivate each other. Review your progress.

When questions arise, reread the chapter that can help you stay on track.

Wherever you are, start there!

And remember: Dream big! Work hard! Laugh often!

AFTERWORD
by Kendra Motske

After reading this book you may be saying to yourself, "Sure, Jeff, easy for you to say!" And though he does have a thriving financial planning company and I do have a degree in business/economics, those factors alone do not account for our ability to build a sound financial house together. Yes, they certainly help, but I contend it's more the result of hard work, sacrifice, discipline, communication, and a willingness to live within our means. We started off no differently from many of you: two young twenty-somethings making our way in the world. As life's challenges presented themselves, financial and otherwise, we tackled them head on, *together*, and continue to do so today. We talk. We plan. We share. We adjust. We dream. I can attest to the fact that we truly practice what Jeff preaches. Our story is meant to inspire you to take action, to make changes, to communicate more and to quarrel less. As I often tell our kids, life is a series of choices. So you can *choose* to continue spending too much or to remain in the dark about your financial affairs or to go on making important decisions apart from your spouse, but those choices will *not* put you on the path to financial compatibility. Instead, choose to be disciplined, choose to be more informed, choose to work as a team. Small changes lead to bigger ones. And, God willing, the positive steps you take today will lead to a happier home life and a healthier financial future.

ACKNOWLEDGMENTS

To all of my clients, thank you for allowing me to use your stories in order to help others. Your names and some details have been changed to protect your identity, but you know who you are, and our journey together helped inspire me to write this book.

So many people have helped me through the writing process. I am eternally grateful to my lawyer and friend Mark Lewis for his invaluable insights on estate planning, elder care attorney and gerontologist Susan Geffen for her thoughts on assisted living, Utah State University Professor Jeffrey Dew for sharing his research on how finances affect relationships, and Purdue University Professor Michael Campion, who spent countless hours with me evaluating the compatibility quiz. Nick Richtsmeier is the brain behind the graphics featured in these pages; he also advised me on several chapters. Sean Covi, my insurance and Social Security guru, provided endless information. My good friend and colleague Ron Butt contributed his industry knowledge and keen insight. Danny Chong helped with research. And thanks to the generosity of attorney Harlene Miller, I was fully able to articulate the nuances of bankruptcy. Shannon Ryan is the hero behind my chapter on children and money; Frank Groff and Kristin Hinman are, quite literally, responsible for this book (and for the fact that you are reading it). Without them I would never have found my outstanding agent, Kirsten Neuhaus, whose patience, guidance, and wisdom never ceases to amaze me. She, in turn, led me to my editors, Dan Ambrosio and Claire Ivett, who helped me shape, focus, and generally enhance the manuscript. Abby Ellin spent hundreds of hours reading, editing, finessing, and (gently) chastising me for my excessive use of exclamation points—and she made me laugh while doing so. I am indebted to you all.

Of course, none of this would matter without my parents, Steve and Mary, for the values they instilled in me growing up; my son, Tanner, and daughter, Brooklyn, for never complaining when Dad was stressed about meeting deadlines—you are my pride and joy; and finally, my wife, Kendra—you are my everything! This book is dedicated to you.

NOTES

1. Michelle Singletary, "Before Trouble Hits, Couples Must Be Open About Spending," *Sun Sentinel*, August 13, 2001, http://articles.sun-sentinel.com/2001-08-13/business/0108100715_1_poor-money-management-financial-goals-couples.

2. Jeffrey Dew, Sonya Britt, and Sandra Huston, "Examining the Relationship Between Financial Issues and Divorce," *Family Relations* 61, no. 4 (October 2012): 615–628.

3. I created the War of the Wallets quiz in 2012. Since then thousands of couples have used it.

4. Dan Zadra and Kristel Wills, *5: Where Will You Be Five Years from Today?* (Seattle, WA: Compendium, 2007).

5. Angela Johnson, "76 Percent of Americans Are Living Paycheck to Paycheck," CNNMoney, June 24, 2013, http://money.cnn.com/2013/06/24/pf/emergency-savings.

6. For information on bankruptcy law, I conducted several telephone interviews with Harlene Miller, a bankruptcy lawyer in Orange County, California.

7. Consumer Credit, Board of Governors of the Federal Reserve System, September 2014, www.federalreserve.gov/releases/g19/current; Tim Chen, "American Household Credit Card Debt Statistics: 2014,"

NerdWallet, www.nerdwallet.com/blog/credit-card-data/average-credit
-card-debt-household.

8. Sarah S. Jiang and Lucia F. Dunn, "New Evidence on Credit
Card Borrowing and Repayment Patterns," *Economic Inquiry* 51, no. 1
(January 2013): 394–407.

9. "A Dozen Shocking Personal Finance Statistics," *Business Insider*,
June 22, 2011, www.businessinsider.com/a-dozen-shocking-personal
-finance-statistics-2011–5.

10. Lucie Kalousova and Sarah A. Burgard, "Debt and Foregone
Medical Care," *Journal of Health and Social Behavior* 54, no. 2 (April
2013): 203–219.

11. Martin Merzer, "Love Me, Love My Debt? No Way, Poll
Says," CreditCards.com, www.creditcards.com/credit-card-news/love
-relationship-debt-turnoff-survey-1276.php.

12. Tom Luster, Laura Bates, Marcia Vandenbelt, and M. Angela
Nievar, "Family Advocates' Perspectives on Early Academic Success
of Children Born to Low-Income Adolescent Mothers," *Family Relations* 53, no. 1 (2004): 68–77.

13. Ibid.

14. "What Is Your State of Credit?" Experian, www.experian.com
/live-credit-smart/state-of-credit-2013.html.

15. "What's the Price Tag for a College Education?" CollegeData.
com, www.collegedata.com/cs/content/content_payarticle_tmpl.jhtml
?articleId=10064.

16. Lynn O'Shaughnessy, "50 State Universities with Best, Worst
Grad Rates," CBS Moneywatch, October 2, 2012, www.cbsnews
.com/news/50-state-universities-with-best-worst-grad-rates.

17. Kim Parker and Eileen Patten, "The Sandwich Generation,"
Pew Research: Social and Demographic Trends, January 30, 2013.

18. US Census Bureau, June 2014.

19. Parker and Patten, "The Sandwich Generation."

20. Christine Dugas, "88% in Poll Say They're Worried About Retirement," *USA Today*, October 6, 2011, http://usatoday30.usatoday

.com/money/perfi/retirement/story/2011–10–05/retirement-worries
/50676604/1.

21. Normal Retirement Age, Social Security Administration, www
.socialsecurity.gov/OACT/ProgData/nra.html.

22. I had several conversations with attorney Mark Lewis for information on estate planning and living trusts.

GLOSSARY AND WORKSHEETS

401(k)—An employer-provided retirement account that offers the same tax-deferred features and age requirements of an IRA. There are no income limits, and contribution limits are significantly higher than IRAs.

403(b)—Similar to a 401(k), this is an employer-provided retirement account for nonprofit organizations. They are also referred to as a TSA (tax-sheltered annuity).

457(b)—Similar to a 401(k), this is an employer-provided retirement account for government employees, but there is no 10 percent penalty for early withdrawal before age fifty-nine and a half. However, such withdrawals will typically be subject to ordinary income tax.

529—A college savings plan that allows you to put money away on an after-tax basis and grows tax-deferred for the duration of the account. It can be withdrawn for qualified educational expenses tax- and penalty-free.

ABRs (accelerated benefit riders, also referred to as living benefits)— These come in many shapes and forms. These riders allow the policy holder in a life insurance contract to receive benefits before their demise. Most commonly companies will allow ABRs for terminal, critical, or chronic illnesses. The benefits allow for more flexible planning in the event of an emergency or life event.

APR (annual percentage rate)—Typically the percentage a lender will charge on the amount loaned to a consumer. The higher the APR, the more money creditors are taking from you.

beneficiary—The person who receives a death benefit.

bonds—Debt securities. You can think of them like IOUs, and companies with bonds that you own are obligated to pay you interest.

capital gains—The profit from any transfer or sale of an asset. Any gain is the difference between purchase price and sale price.

COBRA (Consolidated Omnibus Budget Reconciliation Act)—This act allows for temporary continuity of health coverage for employees who would lose coverage because of a layoff, divorce, or other life event.

cosigning—An agreement to pay someone else's debt in the event they cannot pay the obligation. A cosigner is often required for individuals with no credit or poor credit.

CPI (Consumer Price Index)—The United States uses this to gauge the state of inflation. It averages the prices of everyday items across the United States and measures the increase or decrease in those prices to give us a numerical value for the effect of inflation.

Dow Jones—The Dow Jones Industrial Average is commonly referred to as the Dow. It's similar to the S&P 500 as an index that reflects the overall health of the markets. It's composed of the thirty largest companies in the market.

employee stock options—These give employees of a corporation the opportunity to purchase at a discounted rate the stock of the company they work for. The employee has the "option" to purchase at the reduced price but has the same ownership interest as someone on an exchange would have if they purchased the stock through normal channels.

estate planning—The process of planning for the administration and distribution of property after you die. Generally it helps avoid confusion for your heirs and makes it easier for you to maintain control of your assets. Estate planning should always include giving authority to trusted decision makers for financial and health care decisions if you become incapacitated. Medical directives or instructions can be put into writing as well as designating legal guardians of your minor children.

ETF (exchange traded fund)—These funds offer access to a broad range of funds with professional management very much like mutual funds. However, key differences are that you can trade ETFs on the major exchanges and that their prices can fluctuate throughout the day like stocks.

face amount, or death benefit—The amount of money a life insurance company contractually agrees to pay your beneficiaries if you (the insured) die during the time period of the contract.

FAFSA (Free Application for Federal Student Aid)—This allows current and prospective undergraduate and graduate students to determine their eligibility for financial aid. It is a conduit to multiple college aid programs on both the federal and state levels.

FICO score (Fair Isaac Corporation Score)—A score the major credit bureaus use to measure your credit worthiness. A score is generated based on your payment history, debt owed, length of credit history, type of credit used, and recent searches for your credit history. The higher your score, the better.

fifty-nine-and-a-half rule—The age you can begin to take money from retirement accounts without any penalties.

fixed annuities—Insurance contracts that provide a stream of income for the annuitant. Guarantees are typically provided for both principal and earnings by the issuing insurance company.

gross income—All of the revenue flowing into your household for tax purposes. Wages (salaries), capital gains, dividends, and interest are the most prevalent. However, there are many other forms of income. Bottom line: it is the amount subject to taxation by state and federal governments.

inflation—The general and gradual increase in the price of goods and services over time. An example would be the price of a postage stamp twenty years ago versus the price of one today.

IPO (initial public offering)—The initial public launch of a formerly private company. It is when a private company becomes public by selling their shares to the public through a stock exchange. IPOs are commonly used to raise money for expansion plans and to allow the initial private owners and investors to "cash in" on their original investment.

LTC (long-term care)—A variety of services to help those with a chronic condition or disability for an extended period of time. Insurance policies are available specifically for this segment of care. There are several variables to consider when purchasing LTC insurance, such as amount of benefit, duration, and type.

market timing—A basic tactical maneuver to get invested in and cash out of the markets at the right times. It requires the investor to take on the unpredictable nature of the markets and added cost for trading into and out of markets.

Medicare—A US federal health program that subsidizes the health needs of people who are over the age of sixty-five or disabled or have collected Social Security for a minimum of two years; who are undergoing dialysis for kidney failure or are in need of a transplant; and/or who have amyotrophic lateral sclerosis (ALS), or Lou Gehrig's disease.

Medigap—Medigap is considered Medicare supplemental insurance. There are an assortment of features and premiums to enhance your Medicare coverage. It's important to work with a professional to determine a combination of supplemental insurance that's right for you.

mutual fund—A pooling of investor assets that are professionally managed by a third party. It can be a combination of stocks, bonds, and cash equivalents. It typically offers a common objective and investment focus. Mutual funds offer flexibility, instant diversification, and access to segments of the market that you might not otherwise invest in. They are priced once a day after the markets close.

NASDAQ (National Association of Securities Dealers Automatic Quotation) system—The largest stock exchange platform in America. It was the first electronic stock market bringing operational costs down to make trading more affordable.

net income—The amount of money left over after you pay taxes. It's the money available in your checking account to run your household and create your game plan.

normal retirement age (NRA)—The age you can receive full Social Security benefits. It is age sixty-five for anyone born in 1937 or earlier. If you were born between 1938 and 1959, your NRA is based on a sliding scale. If you were born after 1959, your NRA is age sixty-seven.

P&L (profit and loss)—A business report created to analyze the profitability of a firm. It's all the revenue (income) minus all the expenses.

PE ratio (price-to-earnings ratio)—A valuation metric that divides the stock's price by its annual earnings.

required minimum distribution (RMD)—At age seventy and a half you are required to begin withdrawing money from your retirement plans. An RMD calculation is computed yearly to determine what percentage of your account balance must be taken out annually.

RIE (retirement income estimator)—A simple calculation based on your living expenses today to show what your retirement expenses might be when factoring in inflation. RIE should be one of the basic considerations when constructing a financial goal for retirement.

ROI (return on investment)—A simple metric used to let the investors know their profit on an investment. The higher the ROI, the better. However, higher ROIs often come with higher risk.

Roth IRA—Allows you to contribute after-tax dollars for your retirement with withdrawals in retirement being tax-free. These accounts are also subject to annual contribution and income limits, the fifty-nine-and-a-half rule, but avoids RMDs as long as the money has been in the account for more than five years.

S&P 500 (Standard and Poor's 500)—An index of the five hundred largest companies in the New York Stock Exchange or NASDAQ. It's frequently used as a model for funds and a barometer of the health of the market.

SEP IRA (simplified employee pension IRA)—Business owners or self-employed individuals often use this kind of IRA to save for retirement. These accounts are subject to the same rules as a traditional IRA but have different set-up and contribution limits and requirements.

seventy-and-a-half rule—The age you *must* begin to take money out of a retirement account, such as an IRA, 401(k), 403(b), etc. Exception: Roth IRAs are not subject to this rule.

SIMPLE IRA (Savings Incentive Match Plan for Employees)—Similar to a 401(k), this IRA has lower contribution limits and a simpler administration. As the full name implies, it requires employers to match when an employee makes a contribution.

stocks—Ownership interest in a company. They are purchased in shares across different exchange markets. Historically stocks have outperformed bonds but they carry more volatility in the market.

tax deferral—Tax deferral occurs whenever you can delay paying taxes to a later date. This is a benefit that some retirement vehicles utilize to enhance the effects of compound interest, allowing more money to stay invested for a longer period of time.

traditional IRA (individual retirement account)—Allows you to contribute money toward your retirement before that money is taxed; this effectively lowers your taxable income. Once in the account, all the earnings and transactions have no tax consequence in your working years and are deferred, or put off, until retirement (or withdrawal). Taxes are due when you withdraw the money. These accounts are subject to annual contribution and income limits, a 10 percent penalty if withdrawn before age fifty-nine and a half, and required minimum distributions (RMD).

variable annuities—Insurance contracts that allow owners to invest in securities while also offering certain guarantees. Unlike annuities of old, variable annuities allow investors access to their principal through a series of withdrawals instead of through annuitization.

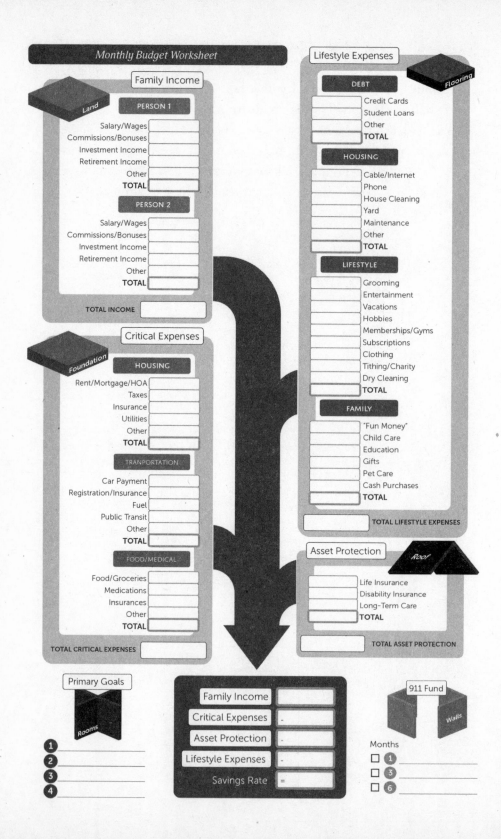

Monthly Budget Worksheet

Family Income

Land

PERSON 1

Salary/Wages
Commissions/Bonuses
Investment Income
Retirement Income
Other
TOTAL

PERSON 2

Salary/Wages
Commissions/Bonuses
Investment Income
Retirement Income
Other
TOTAL

TOTAL INCOME

Critical Expenses

Foundation

HOUSING

Rent/Mortgage/HOA
Taxes
Insurance
Utilities
Other
TOTAL

TRANPORTATION

Car Payment
Registration/Insurance
Fuel
Public Transit
Other
TOTAL

FOOD/MEDICAL

Food/Groceries
Medications
Insurances
Other
TOTAL

TOTAL CRITICAL EXPENSES

Lifestyle Expenses

Flooring

DEBT

Credit Cards
Student Loans
Other
TOTAL

HOUSING

Cable/Internet
Phone
House Cleaning
Yard
Maintenance
Other
TOTAL

LIFESTYLE

Grooming
Entertainment
Vacations
Hobbies
Memberships/Gyms
Subscriptions
Clothing
Tithing/Charity
Dry Cleaning
TOTAL

FAMILY

"Fun Money"
Child Care
Education
Gifts
Pet Care
Cash Purchases
TOTAL

TOTAL LIFESTYLE EXPENSES

Asset Protection

Roof

Life Insurance
Disability Insurance
Long-Term Care
TOTAL

TOTAL ASSET PROTECTION

Primary Goals

Rooms

1 _____
2 _____
3 _____
4 _____

Family Income
Critical Expenses   -
Asset Protection   -
Lifestyle Expenses   -
Savings Rate   =

911 Fund

Walls

Months
☐ 1 _____
☐ 3 _____
☐ 6 _____

Your Financial Game Plan = Your Custom Home

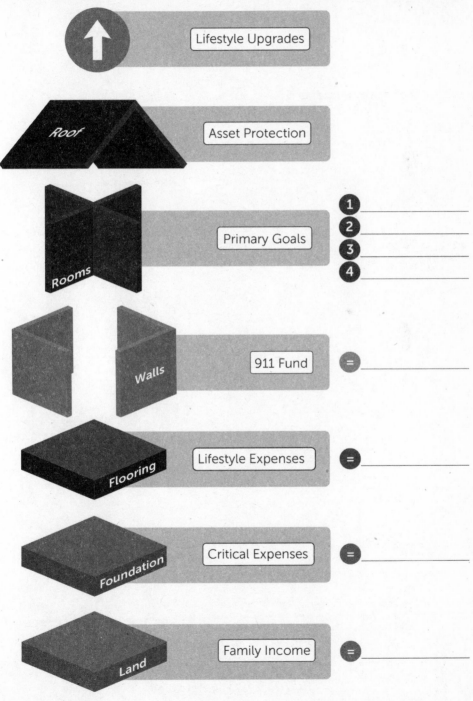

INDEX

A

Accelerated benefits riders
(ABRs), 60, 61
Accounts
access to, 155–156
automatic drafts from, 17
children's, 89–90
guaranteed, 107, 108
individual, xxviii, 8–9
joint, xxviii, 8
for 911 Fund, 8
tax deferred, 137
Addictive personalities, 31
Advisor. *See* Financial advisor
Allowance
children's, 92–93
monthly cash, 16
Americans for Secure
Retirement, 129
Aspirations, 2
Assets
leveraged, 67, 109

life insurance for protection
of, 62
Assisted living facility, 114,
120–121
ATM, using home as, 34
Attorney. *See* Lawyer
Automatic account drafts, 17

B

Bank account, opening for
children, 89–90
Bank statements, reviewing,
16–17
Bankruptcy
Chapter 7, 24–25
Chapter 13, 25
credit card debt and, 24–25
Bonds, 49–50
Bucket list, 143
Budget
child care costs, 80–81
children's, 90–92